FREEDOM TODAY

The Self and Choice in a World of Strict Standards

Fabio Couto

FREEDOM TODAY

The Self and Choice in a World of Strict Standards

Copyright © 2019 by Fabio Couto

All rights reserved. No part of this book may be reproduced or transmitted in any form or by any means, electronic or mechanical, including photocopying, recording, or by any information storage and retrieval system without the written permission of the author, except where permitted by law.

ISBN: 9781798468654

Artwork: Fernando Fidelis

To J, my rock,

the steady, warm hand I never wished to

admit I needed.

"That thing is called free, which exists solely by the necessity of its own nature, and of which the action is determined by itself alone."

—Baruch Spinoza

TABLE OF CONTENTS

PREFACE 11

THE TRAP 33

FREEDOM TODAY 47

WORK 75

LOOK 101

LOVE 129

LIFE ONLINE 155

EPILOGUE 179

ACKNOWLEDGMENTS 193

BIBLIOGRAPHY 197

PREFACE

"Freedom is not enough. What I desire doesn't have a name yet." I was in my early teens when I came across Clarice Lispector's greedy, anxious clamor. Her words echoed loud inside the head of a free-spirited boy raised under the claustrophobic realm of conservative, severe parents, in a small town in the depths of Brazil. Stranded in an environment of strict authority and under imposed definitions of values, convictions and habits, I was sure that freedom was everything a man could ask for. Hurricane Clarice was the Brazilian writer famous for, with precision of vocabulary and style, spitting out the rawest of human emotions with urgency, passion and yet a disturbing ease. It struck me that she wanted more. How powerful—I thought. What else could she possibly desire?

Both my parents came from humble backgrounds, and together, through their hard work, climbed up the socioeconomic ladder when my younger brother and I were growing up. Their paths had direct impact on how we were taught to see the world. While we had the best possible education and plenty of gifts every Christmas, we never took anything for granted. We cultivated simple tastes and habits and grew up hearing about the importance of hard work and personal progress. Our view of the world was provincial. Being free, for my parents, meant improving how we lived through the means of their own effort. Overcoming the restraints of their childhoods to lead a comfortable life. An objective, honest understanding of freedom.

They also taught us, from very early, that we had to be thankful, to them and to God. That we had to study hard and that signs of early development and good grades weren't achievements, but our obligation. That every little toy, every object, every conversation had its exact place to be. That both the house and we were to be kept impeccably tidy, and that crying, along with other displays of emotion, should always be avoided, particularly in front of others. We were taught how to be men within our sexist society. We learned what it meant to be good and to be bad, and pointed to real-life examples of both, based less on people's integrity and more on their appearance or whether they led so-called virtuous lives.

We knew we were not to argue or reason against any of their resolutions and that their decisions needed no explanation. That we had to distinguish, by ourselves, between which of their examples we were meant to follow, and the things only adults could do or say.

How relatives and friends lived or how the world changed around us had nothing to do with our standards and how affairs were run within our family. It didn't matter if anyone was watching something, eating something, going somewhere. We should follow our own, strict set of rules, and always, always ask for permission.

My brother and I were loved deeply, but in silence. There were no hugs, no comforting, no expression of our feelings—or theirs. Until today we both struggle to articulate and talk about how we feel. We were well raised, but suppressed. While brought up to become honest, responsible people, we were forced to fit into our family like pieces of a tangram puzzle, rigid and in pre-determined, precise shape.

All I wanted was freedom—nothing else. In that context of solid control, I dreamt of being fluid, of overflowing, of overcoming. Being free, for me, meant breaking away from a suffocating authority. Liberating from the beliefs that had been imposed on me, from the lack of perspective of living in a small town, from my own innocence and ignorance.

. . .

When I was 18, I came out to myself and to a friend as a gay man. It was the outcome of internal processes lasting years, perhaps my entire life, and it had been painful, as it often is in cases like this. I had left home to study—my father's lifelong support for my intellectual development has always been stronger than the grip of his control. Outside, exposed to new people, possibilities, new ideas, new ways of looking at the world, for the first time I felt that I could look at myself with honesty. I felt confident enough to dismantle my barricade of denial, excuses, of fabricated desires and reach out to hold my own hand. I could claim my identity and my place in the world—even if only to myself and my dear friend Carol.

I felt relieved, embarrassed, ashamed. More than anything, I felt afraid. Terrified of how my parents would react if they ever heard the "news." I remembered clearly—I always will—how they had spent my entire childhood and teens swinging between overlooking and combating the obvious signs my sexuality had presented. I saw my first psychotherapist when I was about four, and she told me amiably that I was there so we could look into why I liked to play with girls and girls' toys—one of those early memories we never forget. And their battle was only starting.

Through the years, of course, I made the obvious, but unconscious connection between those censored behaviors and that secret part of me that started blossoming inside: my sexuality, my affection, my loving. And while the words were never said out loud, I understood that that was something I was not meant to be. I mustn't. It was another rule, a very strict rule, it was our unspoken pact. Their pact. Fearful of the very idea of homosexuality, they spent the years fighting what they saw as its symptoms, with teachers, psychologists, God, and tighter control.

But the subtle, yet loud traces of gayness never yielded, always letting escape, even if for a moment, that inner self that ultimately spilled over and came out entirely to Carol. And I told her when that happened, this is incredibly cathartic, but it's only for a moment. It's not something I'm going to *pursue*. It may be who I am, but it's not how I am going to live, it can't be. I would rather die unhappy than cause such great disappointment to my parents.

She heard quietly, as good friends do, and bought me a book called *The Zahir*, a novel by Brazil's favorite writer-magus,

Paulo Coelho. Zahir means 'obvious' in Arabic, and in the novel, it represented an overarching set of unwritten rules passed from one generation to the other dictating how we should live. It follows us from birth, throughout our childhood, all the way until death, and it determines our behavior and our every move based on the assertions of the many who came before us. *The Zahir* is the clear answer to all questions, and leaves no room for openness or change:

"We must dress according to the dictates of fashion, make love whether we feel like it or not, kill in the name of our country, wish time away so that retirement comes more quickly, elect politicians, complain about the cost of living, change our hairstyle, criticize anyone who is different, go to a religious service on Sunday, Saturday or Friday, depending on our religion, and there beg forgiveness for our sins and puff ourselves up with pride because we know the truth and despise the other tribe, who worships a false god.

"Our children must follow in our footsteps; after all we are older and know about the world. We must have a university degree even if we never get a job in the area of knowledge we were forced to study.

"We must study things that we will never use, but which someone told us was important to know: algebra, trigonometry, the Code of Hammurabi.

PREFACE

"We must never make our parents sad, even if this means giving up everything that makes us happy.

"We must play music quietly, talk quietly, weep in private, because I am the all-powerful Zahir, who lays down the rules and determines the distance between railway tracks, the meaning of success, the best way to love, the importance of rewards."

Shortly after coming out, I returned home after a whole year away, and on my first night back my father asked me if I was gay. I don't think I had ever heard him say that word. With my barricade still dismantled, I gasped for air and felt like I had no choice but to answer "yes." My father had chosen coming out for me. Looking back, I think that in a way it was compassionate, stripping me out of the agony of making that decision, of maybe years of claustrophobic closet life.

My memory of that night is erratic and confused. There were tears and screams, doors being slammed, resentment and the baring of all those feelings we spent our lives not talking about. It felt like the world was crumbling beneath our feet. But it was even harder to wake up the morning after and realize that it hadn't, and ourselves and our suffering were there still.

Time made things less dramatic, but not the slightest less emotional, sad. My father didn't speak to me for months, while living under the same roof. My mother was torn between her firm beliefs, and her maternal, unconditional love for a suffering son. Mothers love differently. My brother, a teenager at the time, couldn't understand why there was so much drama over something that had always been so obvious, what was all that fuss about?

Myself, I ached and healed, feeling unsupported and misplaced, while finally closer to a life with no denial. Being free now only meant being myself, and it still meant everything.

. . .

When I reached my early 20s and started college, I was living alone in a big city, fresh horizons, surrounded with like-minded people. I had fun. I felt more comfortable with myself, perhaps even confident, and had established a good relationship with my parents, who supported me; nothing brings families closer together than long geographic distances. I had become aware of, perhaps I even got to actively shape who Fabio was, and it was time to throw him out into the world.

But I knew the work was far from over. Through my childhood and teenage years, I had built up an avid sense of independence, and I needed desperately to rely on my own tools and resources, to stand on my own feet. I strived, I yearned to gain control of every aspect of my own life, every decision. Not to ever ask for or follow guidelines and advice but just to move forward on my path, alone.

I worked and dreamt of my financial independence, the ultimate assurance of not being under anyone's authority, but also proof that I had made it! I wouldn't need anything else. I studied at a good university and read a lot—I knew that to face the world, I first needed to know it. I had been taught and firmly made to believe that only by being informed, educated, only with my eyes fully open could I make my own choices and be truly free. Ignorance had never been an option.

This was a phase of intense experimentation and discovery, of testing my possibilities and those of life and the world and feeling both afraid and empowered to go after what I wanted. Of course, I had no idea of what I wanted. More than ten years have passed and I still don't.

At the time, I didn't realize that I was also growing lonely. Coming from a place where I never felt comfortable exposing my weaknesses or reaching for help, while obsessed with the idea of an all-embracing independence, I started shutting people out. Holding on to a sense of inviolable intimacy, proud of my projected ability to lead and manage my life all by myself, I became more reserved and less charismatic. I almost transformed into a properly serious person. I loved, and was close to my dear friends, but always kept part of me only to myself.

My first romantic relationships were distant, filled with fear of involvement as I resisted making space for other people in my life—what happens to the sense of self you carefully built if you let people in and they end up staying? And I started unconsciously choosing certain aspects of my personality that I allowed people to touch, always with caution, never fully opened up, taking in more and sharing less. It made me feel safe. It took a while to realize that it also hurt.

I held tight to my independence, rationalizing that freethinking and a life with no interference are invaluable. But I suppressed my human need (and ability) to engage with other people—also invaluable. Freedom can be tricky. I built and reinforced an image of self-sufficiency, of hard effort working towards perfection. And I strived to fulfill it, to fulfill myself. I moved forward with a kind of trembling confidence, learning more about myself and the world, trying to understand and accept my flaws and my shortfalls.

Becoming an adult is a curious process, subtle and abrupt. There's a casual yet steady progress. You learn not to burn your food, to take care of your finances, to heal your own heart. But then you reach a cliff, you're hit by a sudden epiphany, when you realize you hold full responsibility for everything, despite feeling

PREFACE

so unprepared. Somewhere between a first job, uncertainty about the future, vacation and filing taxes, we discover ourselves as fully independent grownups. And when you get there, does it finally set you free?

. . .

Growing up in a small town made me obsessed with the vastness of the world and discovering it for myself. My grandparents and all those prior to them had only worked and lived in the country. My parents and their siblings were the first generation raised in urban environments: small towns in the 1960s and 70s. Generations and generations before me had only ever been there, hiding between the mountains of Minas Gerais, a landlocked state in the southeast of Brazil tracing back to colonial times. The entire world as we knew it, and it was enough. For them, not for me.

    I dreamt of how much life there was to be seen out there—not only multiple languages and food, but entirely different social arrangements, ways of living completely unheard of. Artists, Berbers, monks, aboriginals. For me, just their mere existence was fascinating. Coming to learn of everything that it was possible to be, becoming aware of the universe that extended far beyond that town.

Certainly my inadequacy, my inability to be myself at home had a lot to do with my interest in the outside. But I think there was more than that: since I was a child, my dream wasn't simply of being somewhere else. I dreamt of *always* being somewhere new. What a feeling must it be, to arrive at a place where you don't know anyone, any of their rules, where you may not be able to communicate, complete oblivion turning every step into a discovery. No habits, no conventions, just the uninterrupted taste of the new.

At nine I started studying English. When I was in my early teens a movie called *The Beach* came out, starring Leonardo DiCaprio. It materialized everything I had always dreamt of. He said: "This is where the hungry come to feed. For mine is a generation that circles the globe and searches for something we haven't tried before. So never refuse an invitation, never resist the unfamiliar." And watching that movie, I realized that I hadn't been fantasizing. That it was actually possible to get out there and see the world, to keep looking at it, touch it, breathe in and look at the smile on the faces of people of all colors, with or without teeth, of any or no belief.

Later on, after I left home, I started feeling that same discomfort with the place I had lived in for a while. I had a feeling that what I needed from it was that first excitement of arrival and not ties with people and habits, not belonging to a community. And it was then it became clear to me that the feeling of true belonging is something you can only develop in your early years. And if, for whatever reason, you don't feel intimately connected to that primary unit of living—home, family, place—you can never really feel connected to anything else. If the bond of birth, of first existence and comfortable familiarity isn't strong enough to hold you somewhere, nothing else will ever be. And once you leave, there will be forever weakness in any other reason to stay.

Brazilian Rabbi Nilton Bonder made waves when he published his book *Our Immoral Soul*. It claims that, contrary to common belief, we are not made of immaculate souls that are moral compasses to our sinful human bodies. We are rather bodies that have been tamed by tradition, religion and social norms to become moral, while our souls, free from mundane pressure, are transgressive, rebellious and immoral.

In that book he describes the concept of "narrow places," spaces or situations that were once comfortable and provided us with the opportunity to develop, but after we grow and evolve become tightening and impeding. Think of a mother's uterus. The body, set in its ways and with no knowledge of anywhere except that narrowing location, position or habits, resists movement as it feels pushed out. Meanwhile the soul, immoral and unafraid, marches into the unknown, guiding the body and the self into new possibilities, discovery, and a wider space.

Those misunderstood, marginalized, nonconformists, the poor, notes the Rabbi, are better equipped to pack their bags and move towards evolution, while the well-adapted will turn to "ideology, morals, or theology" to justify their wish to stay in the narrow place.

And after years living in that same city, I felt this urge to leave it behind, ready to go somewhere new where I could satisfy my nature of experiment. The destination didn't matter—all I could think about was movement. A burning need not to *be* somewhere else, but to *go*. Hungry for departure. I left, finally, and since I have lived on four continents, in six countries, more than ten different cities. What else can you call freedom, if not knowing, at any time, that you're able to pack your bags and to just go?

. . .

One day I found myself with a lot of what I had wished for. My much prized independence, good relationships with friends, family and myself, feeling loved. Perhaps for the first time I

PREFACE

didn't feel I had to run, that pressure to escape unsettledness. But when it finally came the time to live and I still couldn't feel fulfilled, happy, I discovered anxiety. It is where restlessness lies when you have everything.

It is a complex feeling to describe. Living feels like an infinite wait, after you've learned that no one's coming. It is a constant certainty that everything is leading towards ruin, the lack of hope, a fearful obsession with imagining and preparing for the worst case. It feels like grey skies, a numbing sadness, life unsaturated, no color or joy in any previous source of pleasure.

And it feels like it is forever, there won't be a way to escape, thick chains fastening tight to the absolute lack of perspective. How can you run away from your own mind? Release yourself from the constant presence of your thoughts?

I was unhappy and unexcited, dull, unable to enjoy any moment or experience. Going through life on autopilot.

Afraid, uneasy, and ultimately exhausted from expecting a dark future. Suffocated, yet resigned, unaware of any way in which I could switch off my own head and find some peace.

While waiting for something, like a flight or the time to go somewhere, or on a quiet, unsuspicious Sunday evening; under crisis, my heart would race and I couldn't breathe, and I wept in despair, my full body taken over by the restlessness of my mind.

For a very long time I suffered quietly, confused and ashamed. How could I possibly not control my own wildly-running head? Succumb to it? Is this weakness? And I started wondering if, perhaps, I was finally facing the meaning of ultimate freedom. Liberating yourself from the limitations of your own mind, the ties that bind to suffering, to sorrows, to unexplainable sadness. But it was very clear that self-separation was unattainable. That you cannot go ahead, unless you reach for help. Unless you help yourself.

And it has been a long journey to recognize and reconcile with the complexity and the fragility of my own psyche. To understand that every state of mind, the best and the worst, is temporary, to accept that there is no such thing as self-sufficiency and that, alone, we are not independent and brave but helpless and weak.

With time and some support, you start having more sunny days, feeling less afraid, establishing a better grasp over your own occasional agony. Sometimes I even wonder if I'm feeling not the reflexes of a long-lasting condition but legitimate distress, the weather in the winter, unmet expectations. Not my own erratic mental state but just a symptom of the frail nature of humanity.

But does it even matter? Isn't all suffering legitimate? I cannot tell where my angst is just part of the natural upsets of living and where it becomes a product of the dysfunctional mind I cannot get away from.

In the absence of answers, of fully understanding the source of my unrest, one day it occurred to me that perhaps the solution didn't involve the impossible task of breaking away from my own mind. It couldn't possibly. Perhaps the solution was the rather simple habit of embracing it. I realized slowly that the anxiety didn't come from being trapped within the bounds of my thoughts, but in trying and failing to run away from them. To distance myself from that natural condition of being. And the more you try, the more you realize you can't, the more you feel trapped, the more anxiety. I am coming to understand that we must accept, understand, forgive, praise, fight for, hold tight to our less-than-perfect essence. That is the ultimate freedom.

The world makes that hard. Throughout our entire lives, an image of the ideal being is projected on us. It is transformed and reinforced, a continuous effort by our society to make us fit appropriately in its complex engine. To operate with precision and no error, within certain standards, working towards the same goals—or how else could the world function?

In that process, we are pushed away from our unique, but deficient individual weirdness, our intimate aspirations, the essence of ourselves. We think that standard is just life as it is, without realizing it is life as it has been determined it should be.

We never realize that following is optional—and also devastating.

The fact is, we spend our lives looking for meaning. A tiring, tireless search for meaning, a reason to be. We forget that meaning only exists within our own subjective experience. Trying to find it elsewhere, in collective definitions of happiness, of successful living, of the good life, is not just a distraction. It is the denial of what we, as individual human beings, subjectively stand for. It restrains, it curbs, it fastens tight.

Throughout my life, the idea of freedom has hunted me. Can we really desire anything else? And can we ever really get there? I have spent hours through the days, through the years wondering, without coming to anything close to a definitive conclusion. But we don't think to reach conclusions—we think for the wonder of the process. And the new ideas that spark along the way.

These notes don't aim to come up with a revolutionary approach to life, and they don't introduce any groundbreaking lenses through which we should look at our social relationships. I have no intention to provide a recipe for happiness, or to go on an anthropological discussion on the taming power of society. These are just a reflection on people in the world we live in, based on my own experience as a human being. My frustrations, my insecurities, my struggles and my pleasure. And those of my friends, family, and people I observe. I am learning, through my own empirical evidences, that getting closer to our essence, to our own nature, turning away from whatever else, if not the path to perpetual bliss, at the very least makes living more fun.

. . .

Some time ago I met a true bohemian, a contemporary hippie with eyes full of life and the carefree smile of a child. I later came to call him Puppy, because his joy and energy reminded me of an active lab puppy with a wide-open mouth, wagging his tail in an innocent lurch. On our first date we talked about shamanic healing rituals, adventures in the open sea and feeling the earth on the ground in a distant life, far from the city and close to the wild. We were talking happily when he suddenly stopped and looked me in the eye, as weird people like that do, and asked point-blank: "Fabio, are you free?"

I could tell he wasn't asking if I was free right then to stay together for longer, or if I was available, uncommitted. The hippie wanted to know if I was a free creature, if I had no restraints and no ties, if I felt free. For a second I sat stunned, recapturing the series of meanings to freedom I had encountered through life. How I had tirelessly pursued freedom, only to watch it change form. From the perspective of that boy growing up, I was certainly free: a grown, relatively successful man, in charge of my home, my body and my life, carrying sole responsibility for each of my decisions with no attaching bonds to people, to a piece of land or any place, no debt. A wild heart living in an open cage. Was that freedom, though? There were no ties or boundaries restricting my ability to come and go, but there was certainly a powerful voice determining my direction of travel. Was it possible to liberate from years of built-up expectations, standards, idealization and external constructs of a good life and happiness? Could we *ever* be truly free?

I giggled, replying insecurely, "Of course I am!" He and I moved on to become friends, but his question never stopped burning in my head and my heart. In a way it always had.

Puppy, here is my best attempt to answer it.

THE TRAP

From the day we are born we are taught beliefs, values, and adequate behavior. We observe living standards, and we are exposed to common sense. We learn the collectively established meanings of right and wrong, punishment and reward, of failure and pleasure, of success, of happiness. From our earliest days and throughout childhood, our parents, extended family, teachers, friends, religions, and the media start shaping how we see the world and ourselves.

Those views—their views—will ultimately go on to determine our aspirations, our judgment, and our perception of value. We learn how we must look and behave in front of others and when it is and isn't appropriate to express our feelings. Soon enough, we learn that there is an adequate way to present ourselves at every occasion, and when we meet other kids in school and are exposed to mass entertainment, our early interactions will start dictating which toys, food, and clothes we want—a very early introduction to fashion and consumerism.

Our entire understanding of the world and of our own existence, from the earliest stage, is shaped by these values that we are taught, the examples we observe, and through comparisons between ourselves and others. The constructs that influence our views during our childhood and early teens are then projected into future plans and projects.

By observing their parents, children learn that growing up, they must find a spouse. The example they observe at home, already at that time, often determines what should be the dynamic and the rules governing their own relationships decades in the future.

They give spontaneous, astronaut-type responses when they're asked what they want to be. But those answers give way to more sober, doctor-like choices as they enter their teens. At that stage, they have understood that everyone must pursue a university degree. They feel engulfed by the career restrictions of the real world and the expectations of their families. Influenced by the media's often inaccurate portrait of professions, the career plans of others around them and the values of the money-driven world we live in.

There is absolutely nothing wrong with learning about the world from our parents and our interaction with others—shared meaning and the transmission of knowledge is the basis for civilization and the only way we can live in society. However, we incorporate these values, beliefs, social norms, and unconsciously use them to build the framework to plan and lead our own lives. A model that we strive to follow, and then use to measure our accomplishments, assess our satisfaction, and determine whether we're happy. It becomes the script of our life. We start accepting that model and those values as if they were the norm, as if they were the right way to live. The only way to live. Even worse: we start believing that the drivers of that life script are our own, that they somehow represent our individual path to a life of happiness and fulfillment.

It occurred to me somewhat suddenly that some of the things I had strived to get or had been forcefully looking for did not really interest me. I held strong to certain values that were meaningful for my parents (stability and achievement) or that I learned from the environment I grew up in (the need to perfect how I look) even though they didn't do much to bring me joy. And I noticed that many others transformed as I moved across different geographies and social circles—money as the appropriate metric of one's achievement, success, worthiness; or the need for love in a grown man's life. Even my preferences, tastes, what I ate, wore, watched, changed in accordance to the tastes of people around me. That contrast—between the values that didn't make me happy, but I still kept, and the ones that transformed, because clearly they didn't mean much—opened my eyes to a life built on parameters entirely outsourced.

We look, dress and talk in a certain way to identify with our social group. We establish a career, preferably a stable, traditional one, and progress in it. We make money, eat healthy, own a house, travel on holiday and make more money, and we must meet someone by the time we are 30 or 35, at the latest (the threshold is stricter if you're a woman), marry them and have children. We should not dye our hair blue, or pierce our nipples, or wear crocs. We shouldn't jump from one job to the other, even if we decide that we want to just keep learning and exploring. We should never let go of ambition and the drive to be more and better. We shouldn't live like hippies, we shouldn't watch reality TV, we should not grow old alone.

My life script and my concerns have always been somewhat traditional, guidelines that direct many in our world today. But they aren't universal: they change according to geographies, social-economic backgrounds, all the way down to the specific communities we grow up and live in. **What is**

universal is the fact that everyone, everywhere is planning their lives, making choices and measuring the importance of their achievements based on principles we build through social experience only, without listening to our hearts.

A friend in her early thirties has spent the last fifteen years traveling the world, satisfying her need to experience places, cultures, and the restlessness of her soul. She currently talks about an intimate, hidden wish to settle down, and dreams of little wonders she envisions in a stable life she hasn't built. However, the idea of stability scares her, and she talks with reservation of the "craziest" thing she ever thought about doing: studying to be a doctor. She wonders, puzzled, what such a dramatic change in course would mean. Being wild became her signature mark, what she is known and admired for, and she doesn't want to be seen as adjusting to that obvious lifestyle of the rest of the world—even if that's what her heart is now asking for. While most people are forced into a life of stability, the script she built allows for none of it, even though she might now want some. External expectations in conflict with the wishes of the heart.

Another example: while most of the people I know today are very keen to consume anything that they consider to be luxurious or expensive and engage with the feelings of power, achievement, and the belonging that the fancy brings, my parents reject everything that they perceived to be refined. They are strict about, for instance, not even trying any food that they think sounds sophisticated. They don't know whether they like it. It has less to do with the taste they developed through life than a concern with the signals they are sending to themselves and to those in their social circle. They seem unconsciously terrified of being associated with any of the habits of an elite that they don't exactly admire, and where they don't want to belong. Those external expectations, influencing our human experience.

Values and standards change from context to context, and they also change within us over time, influenced by the transformations of the world and by the people we surround ourselves with. The pressures we put on ourselves change, and the parameters that we use to measure our satisfaction or happiness do too. As we absorb new standards and compare ourselves to new people, we are always reshaping our idea of what and where we should be. Quite often, these changes involve realizing the irrelevance of some of our previous concerns, only to find new shortcomings to punish ourselves over. From getting into university, to getting laid, to getting that job, to getting married, to staying married, to getting hard...

How often do I hear, from others and within myself, of choices, conscious or unconscious, made to address expectations, please family and friends and to become the individual we want others to look at? A friend who thinks she must marry a certain guy because he "ticks all the boxes." Career decisions made because "it will look good on my resume." While following different models and different values, and reshaping them through time, we are all ruled by an understanding of the world ultimately determined by principles that were established externally. They have absolutely no regard for our own individuality.

. . .

With a life script and values established, we will then strive to fit in and to achieve the goals that have been determined for us. They become our guidelines, our dreams, and in that process, they further suppress our own drivers and instincts. We are born to process the world both based on external stimuli and the intrinsic reflections we bring into the cognitive process, but the dynamic of adulthood and everyday life gradually shuts down our inner voice to follow the script.

We no longer know how we really want to live, or where we want to get—we don't even realize that there are other ways, other paths, hundreds of possibilities. There is no openness or willingness to experiment and discover the new. We often won't even acknowledge that there might be anything new, the possibility of different life choices.

I spent years working hard to move around the world and experience different places. To keep discovering. Carving myself the opportunities to explore and to be able to live well while repeatedly starting from scratch. The changes were never easy, but they did feed my soul. But I reached an age and a point in my career where I felt I had to start growing roots. When people around you begin settling down and creating families it becomes harder to break into an entirely new, well-established social context, all on your own. You watch them build their homes, emotional structure, networks of support. And you start to believe you should be getting yours too. I had made it to London from nowhere, and the journey hadn't been easy—that in itself had to be a sign of mission accomplished. A requirement for settledness. That had to be it.

So when I started feeling unhappy and misplaced, it felt like it was my obligation to make things work one way or the other. I had to insist, fill the holes, calm my heart down. Find another job, meet different people, make it happen no matter how. That was what was right. It was appropriate. I couldn't keep going around forever, I couldn't wish or ask for more. The time for discovery had passed. And I tried hard and put up with so much unhappiness because I was clinging to this idea of how life is supposed to unfold. That perspective I had learned growing up, and further developed as an adult had shut down my instinct, and dictated when was the right time to live, and how.

But the years didn't matter, there was a Fabio who was still there, whose thirst didn't fade or age, who enjoyed it, who craved fresh air and who might never, ever become too old to break camp. I had just temporarily shut my eyes and my ears to him.

Faced with a choice between the death penalty and resigning from the study and teaching of philosophy, under trial for "corrupting" the minds of his students, Socrates coined his maxim: "An unexamined life is not worth living"—before being killed. Greeks before him already preached self-discovery as a way of life, commanding: "know thyself." Knowing ourselves is, indeed, the only way to differentiate what we've been taught that matters, from what really does, to us.

On the contrary, we find ourselves in a self-enforcing dynamic: we don't try to investigate our values and wishes because there is already an established framework that we think we must follow, and we keep ourselves within the boundaries of that framework because we are not aware of our own, distinct values and wishes. We go through our entire lives disconnected from the essence of our nature. Trapped in that cycle, we direct all of our efforts and energy to following the script, striving to achieve the milestones that we think determine whether we're accomplished.

We want to have other people's definition of a "good life," whatever that means in a given context. It sort of goes like this: we know that at a certain age we should be graduating and starting a career. By that time, we should either have met our future spouse, or be doing that soon: getting married is the next step. We will have and raise children while getting promoted, hopefully, and later we might get a divorce, or not—the divorce just recently became an accepted possibility. If we do get divorced, there's a specific type of person we should be looking for to fill the position of the first one, after all we've reached a certain age. In any case, what we are really looking for is retirement, the much-expected chance to enjoy that delightful life we've built.

Change the script all you want, in one form or the other, it's always there. The expectations by which we live are always there. We dedicate our lives to chasing after things which we are not sure whether we really want. It is so obvious that it goes without saying, but **it is not possible to find fulfilment without understanding what it is that fulfils us**.

. . .

The lack of awareness over our own motivations and the pursuit of collectively established goals traps us: people who manage to achieve those goals realize that, after a lifetime of work and energy, they still feel incomplete. Those who don't are frustrated, often doubling down on their efforts to fit in and growing increasingly distant from themselves.

The World Health Organization estimates that 350 million people suffer from depression globally. In the United Kingdom, the National Health Service prescribed antidepressants at a record rate in 2016, jumping over 100% from 2006. A study in the country, The Youth Index, found that people aged 16-25 have never been more unhappy, with 61% feeling stressed, 25% feeling "hopeless" and 50% having experienced some kind of mental health disorder.

Doctors, psychologists, anthropologists and sociologists all argue that we are the unhappiest generation in human history. It's not uncommon to hear of people who have seemingly perfect lives but still feel sad. There is nothing scarier than feeling deeply unsatisfied while everything around you seems perfectly in place, nothing missing. The more accomplished, the more restless. Imagine achieving all that you thought was necessary, and still not feeling fulfilled? All boxes ticked: career, marriage, family, money, physical appearance. If someone has everything and nothing else to pursue, happiness will seem impossible to attain.

Moving further and ahead in life, I started observing that ticking boxes actually led me to feel less fulfilled and just puzzled by how my achievements failed to deliver happiness. That mismatch—not being able to understand what is missing, working hard and reaching your goals but not tasting any joy—is gut-wrenching. To that mismatch I owe all of my anxiety, countless sleepless nights and serial challenges to enjoy, happily, a life truly blessed.

One of the most successful business executives I know, a dear friend, built a stellar career as an economist in Brazil. She has a number of loving friends, a healthy, active lifestyle and looks gorgeous, a strong, tall woman with a big open smile. Now in her late 30s, it upsets her that she isn't married or in a stable relationship. She can't seem to get into one, and now her career and success have become challenges, as the ruling script makes men terrified of powerful women. And what she sees as a big, missing piece makes her question her choices and her attributes as a woman, even though she is, otherwise, incredibly happy and doesn't seem to need a man. Maybe her priorities did change. Maybe her heart found a new dream. Maybe a man is simply perceived to be necessary in the life of a woman.

Assessing our individual happiness by assimilated standards and comparison, we judge our self-worth and our merit based on things we don't even know if we like, want or need.

Studies have suggested a link between authority in the workplace and depression. That CEOs' rates of depression are twice that of the overall population, evidence that having reached the top is far from a synonym of happiness.

On the other hand, many are unhappy and feel terribly unsettled, having failed to meet the standards that they thought make for worthy men and women. When we internalize other's values and ways of living, we also start to believe that our satisfaction is dependent upon those arbitrary artifacts. If we have a stable, responsible life, if we found a partner and built a family, if there's a constant increase in how much money we are making.

We are trapped: we can have it all and feel unsatisfied or feel disappointed by how far we got. We often oscillate between feeling one way or the other. The trap makes it very clear, **there is no way to find happiness chasing goals that are not ours.** We must learn to distinguish between values and aspirations that are genuinely ours from those that have been imposed on us. To identify the things that might resonate with our heads and our hearts, that might satisfy our essence. Otherwise we can never find peace.

FREEDOM TODAY

Most of us in the Western world today enjoy a certain degree of individual freedom: the ability to make our own choices, to come and go, to express our thoughts and vote for our leaders. Many of those freedoms are inviolable values at the heart of the establishment of our nations and our life in society. We refer to ourselves as "the free world," and we genuinely believe that that is where we live. We shouldn't take it for granted. But living in a free world does not automatically translate to being free. There is a more intimate level of freedom for us all to conquer: setting ourselves free from values, standards and aspirations that are not connected with our subjective drivers of happiness. Liberating ourselves from a lifetime of built-up expectations, preconceptions and judgment, becoming aware of our essence.

I believe that the illusion of living freely while we are caged in a mind-set that is alienated from our uniqueness is responsible for a lot of the anxiety and sadness in our current times. Freedom today is being able to rise above the collective understanding of good and bad, and the script that was written for our lives, to cut those social ties and live unrestrained and liberated to connect with our own nature.

American psychologist Carl Rogers developed the humanistic movement in psychology, and a therapy method called the person-centric approach. It is based on the principle that people, in our very essence, are good. We have the natural tendency to be the best we can if we are just free to be ourselves. Freedom is all we need to flourish. I find the concept beautifully encouraging: if we are able to establish environments where people are simply able to be themselves, they'll be great. Period. Notice that there's no change proposed, no re-wiring of anyone's personality or behavior. It's simply letting be. Letting go of the predetermined values and aspirations is unleashing that natural tendency, and is key to realizing our full potential. It is not easy. But if we want to live happily, I don't think there's an alternative.

In my journey trying to better understand myself, I was lucky to stumble upon some insights. Simple, but truly cathartic ideas that are helping me reframe how I think about myself and my life. Helping me become more aware of my idiosyncrasies and of the pressures we put on ourselves on behalf of the world. The ideas that life and the world are a product of our own individual perspective, and the acknowledgment that, ultimately, we can live in any way that we choose to.

. . .

At a time of anxiety, I first started learning about Buddhism and came across their idea, or "awakening," that our suffering isn't caused by the circumstances we are in, but by our own reaction to them. In fact, our entire human experience is a construct of our mind, none of it is objective. Everything we experience, our failures and accomplishments, relationships with other people, our paths through life, do not exist but within our heads.

The notion that I felt unhappy because I was tied to standards that aren't connected to my essence first came to me as I brooded over my many shortcomings, what I perceived—and sometimes still do perceive—to be holes in my life. All the aspects in which I lagged behind the people around me. My relative distance from people and my inability to be more sociable. Not being in a relationship. My huge nose. How little money I was making. The gap between where I was and where I thought I should have been at my age. The list goes on.

Reflecting on my frustrations, I started wondering if, with my mind in full control of my own existence, it was possible to change the parameters to meet current circumstances and feel more complete. If life only existed in my head, I could certainly adjust its standards. This mental exercise completely transformed my perspective on myself and the world. Maybe I'm not the world's most sociable person, but I really enjoy my exchanges with the people I do interact with. And my nose looks kind of great if I look at it from the profile. Perhaps it wasn't necessary to have enough money to burn, but living well, as I did, was more than enough. Maybe I could start to believe that the right place for me to be, at my age, was exactly where I was.

This idea isn't exclusive to the Buddhist philosophy. One of the basic principles of semiotics, the science that studies how we create meaning and communicate, is that we don't have the ability to process any object—whether it's an image, a person, or an idea—in itself, in its pure essence. We can only access our subjective understanding of that object, influenced by our culture, our values, our learnings and our personal view. So if we look at a chair, our cognition accesses the baggage of meaning that we accumulated through our lives to process that chair. That is how we understand that it is to be sat on. In itself, it may not be meant for seating, but to hold a door open. Or decoration. It may well be art. In itself, the chair has no meaning.

In the same way, if we look at a person and think they are beautiful, the environment where we grew up, the standards from our current times, the references we take from the media and our own subjective preferences understand that person as beautiful. They are not objectively beautiful because **there is no objectively beautiful!** Beautiful is a partially social, partially subjective construct.

In anthropology, that idea is called 'social constructionism.' It claims that our understanding of the world is developed through social interactions and shared agreements. Because they are just agreements—and not the world itself—that understanding will change according to time and context. Reality, therefore, is constantly constructed, collectively. Ultimately, there is not an objective world. It requires people to observe it, process it and make sense of it, together.

This may all sound like a lunacy from academics in the humanities, but it happens to be scientific. Quantum theory, in physics, claims that particles transform depending on whether people are observing them or not. Experiments have shown that particles, like photons and electrons, can behave either like matter or waves, choosing which simply determined by *how they are being measured.* In essence, studies prove that, at an atom-level, reality does not exist unless someone is looking at it.

Understanding that is important for two reasons: firstly, it proves that none of the notions that we carry in our minds are universal truths. Ideas of what is good and what is bad, beautiful and ugly, how we should or shouldn't behave, none of it. **The world only exists as we perceive it.** There are no objective measures of value, of what living well means, of worthy or unworthy. Those ideas are fragile social artifacts of our days, not biological truths. The fact that they change so drastically throughout time is evidence of how, on their own, they do not translate to human fulfilment.

Take, for instance, how divorce used to be perceived. Under the social conventions of not long ago, getting divorced was absolutely against the script, a failure, at the very least. It triggered shame, embarrassment, guilt (the consequences here, again, were worse if you were a woman). Today, getting divorced has become less of a catastrophe. People are more accepting of the fact that it is ok for things to come to an end. Everyone has watched children of divorced parents grow to be healthy adults. The social norm is fluid because divorce, or absolutely anything else, is not intrinsically, definitively positive or negative.

And then, consequentially, **what makes anything positive or negative is our own mind.** That puts us in control of how satisfied we feel with our own lives. In control of everything. It allows us to make peace with ourselves—there is no external "happiness and accomplishment authority" measuring how well we are doing through time. There is no well-defined checklist of milestones that will determine our accomplishment and fulfilment as human beings. We are the sole judges of whether we live well or not, and that is powerful. It is the path to feel at peace.

However, we combine external—social, cultural, contextual—factors with our internal, subjective self to experience life and the world. There is nothing wrong with that. Freedom is awareness, it's opening the eyes to yourself and the other. It is becoming conscious of your own nature, collective assumptions, and choosing when to embrace which.

When Pablo Picasso, perhaps the greatest painter of the 20th century, was asked to explain the symbolism of his masterpiece Guernica, he was surprised. "It isn't up to the painter to define the symbols. Otherwise it would be better if he wrote them out in so many words! The public who look at the picture must interpret the symbols as they understand them." Later on, in the 60s, Italian philosopher Umberto Eco developed the idea of the "open work," or how artwork doesn't carry a predetermined, one-way message from the artist to the audience. Instead, it sparks the possibility for multiple understandings, inviting the interpreter to create sense and meaning themselves. Life itself is like an open work of art. We bring our heart and our baggage when we try to make sense and react to it. Freedom is knowing to use both.

. . .

This is as obvious as it is groundbreaking, it is the most beautiful fact about adulthood, so simple, but always forgotten or overlooked: **we can live in any way that we choose to.** Within the limits of the law, civility, and respect for other people, we can do anything. Anything. And then we can change our minds and do differently. Everything is possible, at any time. We have interiorized that life script so deeply that we forget that what we do as adults is entirely our choice.

I was living through one of the hardest moments in my life. Struggling with intense anxiety and fear for the future and spending hours imagining wild, catastrophic scenarios of failure, loneliness, unemployment and shame. But I found an unexpected source of relief for my insecurity. Around that same time I was reading a memoir by performance artist Marina Abramovic, famous for testing the limits of her body and her mind in her artwork through long, physically painful performances. She described discovering that once we reach our limit, at the very extreme of our existence, when all our resources are exhausted and we can no longer take it, when there is no energy left and our own thinking system collapses, we are able to access universal knowledge that surrounds us. When our own brain "checks out"—and only then—we transcend.

In *The Art of War*, Sun Tzu, a Chinese general and war strategist from 500 BC, teaches that, if a commander put his soldiers into a situation with no escape, they would show their strongest force. In the face of death, they could achieve anything. "Soldiers when in desperate straits lose their sense of fear. If there is no place of refuge, they will stand firm."

I had just finished studying and was feeling particularly pessimistic about my professional prospects. I felt unrewarded for my efforts, certain that the future was gloomy, and clueless about my next step. My entire life seemed to be on standby, nothing to look forward to. No answers, no confidence, no clarity. Anxiety drains your last bit of energy. One afternoon I read that a company at which I was interviewing and had what seemed to be my last job lead announced its merger with a major competitor.

With the merger there would certainly be dozens of duplicated roles and a large availability of internal talent.

Certainly cost cuts. My chance was gone. Even if they still were to hire someone, they would take months to organize the new company post-merger and start recruiting again. I could never count on that possibility following the star crash. One can't beat fate. And I thought, now that everything has fallen apart, what am I going to do? With nothing left, no job to pursue, where am I going to go? And I started thinking of my possibilities.

A couple of friends who live on an island in the Philippines who might have some work for me. Volunteer programs. Borrow some money and start a new venture. I had always had a few ideas running in the back of my mind. I could study yoga and learn to live with so much less. I suddenly realized that I didn't *have to* find a job. Or to move forward with my career. The world wouldn't end. No one ever died of unemployment. I certainly needed to work and pay my bills, but the bounds of that constraint are so much wider than we think. There are countless ways of living, and living well, that didn't involve finding that next corporate job. I could never see them because I thought, and often I still think, that there is a predetermined way of leading life. The realization was so cathartic.

The very idea that we must have a career and progress in it is not human, but social. Nothing more than a limiting convention. If we understand that a principle like that isn't intrinsic to ourselves, or in fact to anyone, we can open our eyes to the endless possibilities that life offers.

I say endless because the possibilities I refer to are beyond the life choices that we are already used to making. They are beyond the notions of conventional and unconventional, just getting married or deciding to stay single, having a permanent job or freelancing. I mean full rearrangements of our living, our relationship with ourselves and the world, a reframing of how we engage with life.

Our relationships with our friends, family and the ones we love, the importance of their presence in our lives and the rules of engagement, if you meet once a week, or a year, or ever. If you sleep in the same bed. If you call your mother.

How we think about our future—if we do at all. We may plan, envision, prepare for different scenarios. We can outline goals and strategies to achieve them. Or just invest all of our energy in now, dive into the living experience and save no money. We can choose to lead lives that are structured and stable, with well-established routines, or we can go wherever the wind blows. We can decide whether we are happy or successful, or not, or don't think about that at all.

There are no "have tos." We have full control of our days, our choices, our path. I met three very smart Parisians in a relationship full of love—all three, the same relationship. They have been together for years and call themselves a "trouple." They sleep together (in a special, oversized bed) and make one another happy. They pay absolutely no regard for how other people might perceive their relationship and care only about enjoying their life together. "Doesn't it get messy?" I asked. Two-people relationships already seem to carry more than enough drama. "It doesn't matter," one of them said. "You just get used to it…"

A friend of mine, a beautiful woman now in her early thirties, does not like sex. Never has. She tried it a few times but it's just not her thing. She has no wish to try again, doesn't think about it, doesn't want to find therapies. There's no trauma; she is not into it and lives well without it. Why did that seem so strange? Shouldn't sex be about the individual's pleasure—and nothing else at all?

Another friend has been a 'digital nomad' for years now —essentially working online and moving from country to country. She is an advocate and career coach for the lifestyle. They work remotely from cafes, bars, restaurants or hostels anywhere, and then move on. They are a huge community globally, exploring the world and connecting with the restless nature of their souls, while contributing to the digital economy. A beautiful example, a collective rise against the well-established idea that we must have a home. There is nothing we must have.

I read an interview with young Danish writer Thomas Korsgaard who was asked to describe his feelings with regards to family, to which he replied: "I tried to have one until I was 17 years old, but it's not me." I laughed at his wit. He seemed confident and happy without a family. His choice. We must understand, fully accept that there are simply no "musts" in life.

And on top of being free to live however we want to: being free to transform, one of the most amazing human capabilities. We are never stuck to any route or lifestyle, but always remain free to move on unrestrained, to flow through life and evolve, as is inherent in our human nature. Irish playwright George Bernard Shaw famously wrote, "You see things; and you say 'Why?' But I dream things that never were; and I say, 'Why not?'"

"Why not" to every scenario, every single choice in life, every plan. The wildest dreams and revolutions. New ways of thinking, behaving and ageing. Reinvented paradigms, psychological, emotional or practical. **Why not?**

Now, this is not a suggestion that unconventional lives are the solution for our anxieties or that we should throw everything out in the wind. Sometimes, supposedly unorthodox values can be just as restraining as the traditional pressures of social life. Finding prescriptions to a better life is completely missing the point; the better life only exists within each individual. No one needs to change course or behavior at all; what is liberating is simply knowing that we *can*. It would be easy if the key for happiness was just running away with a circus. Living aware of our endless possibilities as human beings—and not necessarily following any one of them—is what allows us to be free, to be ourselves, to be happier.

In fact, many may find that the established patterns actually suit them quite well. That they enjoy the stability, their loving, conventional marriage, their SUV. That is great, to enjoy and find fulfilment in a lifestyle that is so widely accepted socially. But to be able to truly enjoy even the most traditional choices, you must be aware. You can't truly appreciate the joy your life brings until you understand that that life is your own: not imposed, not pre-established, but yours. And that it includes a perpetually open door for change and transformation.

Back when I first went through this reflection, I felt free because I realized I could always find a way. I could always change my expectations, come up with different goals, make a different plan and move on, move forward. Bringing that notion into consciousness still helps me take pressure off my shoulders when I feel unsettled, restless or afraid. If the game feels too hard, I can change the rules. Or play a different game.

. . .

The scariest part of living is that we only do it once, it is always our last chance. We don't get to write a draft, to make corrections, to try the other choice. We can't come back and fix things. It would seem fair, at the very least, to get a chance to understand what living entails, to study our possibilities and to make a strategy, before the clock starts ticking. But we must try to learn about it as it goes by, and learning is complex while it goes by incredibly fast. How overwhelming does it feel, trying to figure life out while our only opportunity to live it is passing by?

Existentialist philosophers wrestle extensively with the idea of the meaning to life. Albert Camus, in particular, focused his work on a cruel gap in human existence, a gap philosophers call the Absurd: that we keep searching for purpose and meaning in life, while life is inescapably meaningless. Camus is categorical: the universe is random, cold and chaotic. The Absurd is the name of the tireless, but hopeless, human search for meaning in a world that has none.

I always felt like so many questions are left unanswered, the years go by and we are not sure of where we are heading. Time scares us because we can't be certain of whether we are allowed to feel accomplished, whether life has been fulfilled, now or ever. We don't know what true accomplishment even means. Meaning, in itself, is unclear, uncertain, an ever-fleeting abstraction. How often do we wonder: what are we here for? Where are we heading? Are we doing this right? Why do I get up every day? It cannot be just to eat and reply to emails. And while we try to understand, the clock is always ticking.

The current and Third Chamtrul Rinpoche, a Tibetan monk and the 11th in a lineage of recognized reincarnations of traditional scholars and masters from the branch monasteries of Katoch, came to London one night to give a talk on finding happiness in everyday life. I have always been amazed by how carelessly Buddhists speak about happiness. Not with the caution and restraint that would be required to touch on a complex, sacred state of human existence, but with the simplicity of describing an ordinary, very possible condition. Perhaps it is, and the caution makes it complex and distant.

I had always been reluctant to even use the word 'happiness:' to me it seemed so ambitious, hard to even grasp, much less one day attain. 'Contentment' or 'satisfaction' seemed more appropriate. I would have been lucky if I could just find some peace. And freedom.

But Chamtrul Rinpoche had not come to London for a conceptual discussion or to present the Buddhist take on human conditions, he came to teach something very objective: **how to**

find happiness in everyday life. Bold task, I thought. I came to the Vihara—the temple—on a Friday night. There were about 30 people attending. Most also seemed to have come in search of answers. The monk walked in slowly and sat down on a cushion up front. There was a respectful, absolute silence. He looked vibrant, young and full of light, and yet calm and restrained. We sat quietly on metal chairs and he started chanting, beautifully. Everyone was already captivated, connected to his energy and his presence, when he finished the chanting, he paused and then asked, straightforwardly: what is the purpose of life?

It didn't sound like a rhetorical question.

I instinctively arranged myself on my chair and leaned forward, an unconscious attempt to listen better and make sure I didn't miss a single whisper, any of his breaths. I could hardly believe what seemed to be about to happen. The question of all questions, my—everyone's—eternal search. The one that never let you reach investigative satisfaction but only led to more thinking, more questioning, more unsettlement. The uncertainty we live and die with. Could he possibly have an objective answer?

And he replied, still calm, still unexcited: it is to *enjoy* it.

As he elaborated, I sat in slight disbelief, it seemed so unlikely that the most sublime of human agonies could be made so simple, so accessible. That this young monk discussed it so pragmatically in a talk that anyone could have attended, inside the brick and mortar walls of an old temple in Chiswick, West London.

His perspective was simple, but for me it unlocked a whole new understanding of the living paradigm. I had always believed that coming to understand life's purpose was fundamental to feeling fulfilled. That search was the *path* to happiness. Finding the purpose, for me, was a task, and happiness, the outcome of completing it. If I could discover life's meaning, understand what we are here for, it would be possible to accomplish it, and then finally enjoy life.

But enjoying *is* the purpose—not the outcome. That is the meaning of life: pleasure. It is the reason we get up in the morning, why we connect with other people, why we engage with our daily activities: to do so happily. Not to, one day, *achieve* happiness. Happiness can't be the consequence. We live with the pure, simple purpose of enjoying the experience. The notion seemed so obvious, and yet so radical. Most will never realize that we are only here for the pleasure of living, constantly, every minute.

The conclusion of Camus' thinking on the Absurd was not that life, because it's purposeless, is not worth living. He claimed that we are perfectly able to enjoy it if we can just *accept* the Absurd. If we embrace life as it is, devoid of a greater purpose. His idea was also very simple—and too familiar: if we understand the Absurd, if we acknowledge how it determines that the universe has no intrinsic purpose, that it has no absolutes, we can then create meaning ourselves, and live happily. Camus calls that realization freedom.

The monk's talk touched me deeply. For the most part, we neglect happiness. We forget that we can choose happiness. We may be too busy searching for it, too afraid to understand it, to touch it, to even speak of it. Yet that is what we are here for. Since that talk, sometimes, when I notice that I am in a moment of true pleasure, when I find myself, inadvertently, genuinely enjoying something, whatever that might be, I think, now I am living. Only now. Now I am myself. Living up to my purpose. I feel accomplished. And I imagine that, in some other plane, gods and goddesses are looking down and watching me, entertained. They are in awe. They look like young monks and nuns, vibrant and peaceful, and they are laughing in delight, not with me, but at what they observe: a human, living up to the human experience. And I laugh with them.

. . .

Respecting our individuality has another outcome of immense value, another deep personal change it ignites. It is perhaps as important as being able to live better and happier. While making an effort to become more aware of the preconceptions I was using to guide my decisions, I started noticing the other application of collective standards and social hierarchies of value: judging other people. We hold others hostage to the same arbitrary principles that diminish our view of ourselves, creating frustration, anxiety, and a world of unhappiness.

I observed that, at each of my human interactions, from crossing paths with someone on the street, to assessing if a relationship prospect could become a partner for life, I applied assumptions on adequacy, success, and ultimately worthiness. To understand and engage with people, I was using the same assumptions I was trying to reject for myself.

A TED Talk and book by researcher Brene Brown about the power of vulnerability touched me deeply. She claims we must let ourselves be seen entirely, with all our flaws, in order to feel connection to the world and others, and worthiness. Her point is that we need to accept the whole of ourselves, in the full glory of our imperfection, to be able to accept others. When we are kind to ourselves and understanding of our shortfalls, we are able to be kind to others too. I spent my life striving to be perfect. Or more importantly: to project an image of perfection.

Dedicating time and energy to chasing standards of beauty, of professional achievement, of intellectual development—only to feel persistently lagging behind. It couldn't be much of a surprise that I came to be discretionary and judgmental. You must make peace with yourself before you can ever truly open your arms to others. We can feel no compassion unless we are able embrace our own chronic imperfection.

When we understand that certain values and standards aren't ours, but are taught or imposed, we realize that they aren't anyone else's either. They are no one's. And that others, too, should be living in line with what matters to them, exclusively.

Everyone we come across has the right to define their own way of living—what happiness and success mean to them. And they have the right to connect with themselves—their characteristics, fears and aspirations. It is the only way in which they can be happy. When we start to pay attention to our idiosyncrasies, our wishes, we start giving people we interact with the right to do the same. **By accepting ourselves as unique individuals, we learn the importance of accepting others' uniqueness too.** To enforce their right to create their own path.

Reframing our engagement with other people starts with processing the things we see and observe simply for what they are, letting go of the many associations and assumptions we make. What we see is what we see, it shouldn't be anything else.

Any additional sense we try to produce based on an observable trait is unproductive speculation.

People's appearances aren't determinants of their personalities. Being well-groomed doesn't mean being shallow. Signs of wealth, whether clothes or cars, are no indicators of success and personal accomplishment, nor of vanity and arrogance. Things are simply what they are. By understanding that we cannot access the complexity of people, we can stop trying to figure them out entirely and start processing the world as it actually is. It is the door to accepting and welcoming our differences, not only the ones we can observe, but the endless different principles that guide each of our hearts.

Associations and assumptions are natural processes in human cognition. Rational thinking implies categorizing things based on shared beliefs and past experience. They shouldn't, however, serve as the only basis on which we become aware of others. Or be confused with stereotyping.

In this process I came to notice that I had unconsciously established certain parameters for people I was willing to engage with. Within a moment of looking at or talking to someone, I established if they were in any way interesting or not, if I thought they were worth my time. So I went on to investigate the habit. Thinking in retrospect on the people who provided my best, most pleasant moments with other humans. My goal was to understand if I was instinctively looking for people who were similar, who shared key characteristics and could replicate my past, positive experiences with others.

It turned out that, in fact, some of the most incredible people I had met, the ones who had an impact on my life, were actually did so quite unexpectedly. Often dramatically different from any obvious, striking stereotype. They were stimulating and weird, and unveiled themselves slowly, in ever-more exciting layers, turning out to be so different from my flawed first impressions. Exciting people, full of life. They introduced me to new habits and thinking, and certainly had nothing to do with the predictable, me-like profiles I saw myself focusing on. My screening process for new people was terrible. It had no basis on my previous experiences, no connection with those I actually enjoyed being around. It was full of automated, misguided judgment.

Looking at people open-heartedly, entirely free from assumptions and social parameters, isn't easy. It may not even be possible. Categorizing is a natural process, and it's helpful; our brain simply doesn't have the capacity to process completely new subjects constantly. It has to refer back to its catalogue of experiences. Turning that off entirely isn't feasible or helpful.

Changing the approach is rather a constant exercise. It starts simply with observing our thinking patterns and noticing how we perceive others—the hidden associations, preconceptions—and consciously setting them aside to open up to people and to the world. If we open our eyes and accept that we all come from different places, that we are driven by different motivations, we can stop looking at people as we or the world think they are, and simply let them be. Their true selves are always more interesting than the boxes we put them into.

. . .

While planning my intimate, personal revolution against all standards, I observed the clash between how I was starting to understand happiness and a world where people seem increasingly keen to judge, to impose morals, to demand outlined conduct and behavior, and hold tight to convention and tradition, not only for themselves, but as requirements for everyone.

What does it mean, I wondered, for my thoughts to come out at a time when people feel, more strongly than ever, that their beliefs are absolute truths and their world view must be followed and enforced?

John Stuart Mill is considered the father of liberalism. His work in politics and social sciences were centered around his idea of liberty, or the right of individuals to choose for themselves, as opposed to the then-existing ideas on the power and control of the state. His most famous work, *On Liberty* (1859), proposed strictly restricting the influence society, or the government, or external forces should be able to exert on the individual.

He became known for the implications of his work on social structure, law and the tension between power and people. But I am interested in a more intimate reading of his thinking, the underlying belief that underscored his perspective: the beauty and the power of individual choice.

Mill's first book, *A System of Logic*, was not about the social or political sciences, but philosophy of science. In other words, how to produce knowledge and science. He presents the foundation for all of his thinking: that speculation, individual understanding, questioning, is the path to progress. He refuted blind belief in conventions, transferred knowledge and tradition, and argued that the individual should be exposed to all possible ideas, challenge all of them, and make up their own mind. That is the only way to drive humankind forward.

Some people today might see the idea that we should disregard social conventions and follow our own paths as a threat to their traditional take on life, our existing social contracts and the structure of our communities. These people are everywhere. They are terrified. They tremble before any movement that suggests that the world is not in its perfect place, that we must change and look ahead, that we are transforming, inevitably. That "progressive" is not a political perspective but a defining attribute of history.

If we just throw away centuries of built-up expectations and carefully constructed life trajectory, where will we end up? If everyone starts living however they want, if people stopped caring about promotions and careers and stopped measuring others' value in financial currencies? And if girls stopped dreaming of getting married and women dressed and behaved however they liked? If each individual stopped referring to collective understanding and started thinking for themselves, would we just live in total chaos? Where would society, where would the world go? Almost two centuries ago, Mill provided the answer: they would go forward.

It is through discontent, and not obedience, that we can propose better ways of living. It is only by challenging the status quo that we are able to think of improvement. And it is by listening to ourselves, by investigating, that we become discontent. That we think of solutions, of a better world. As individuals, it is not our responsibility to uphold the existing social order. We have no commitment to the appropriate functioning of society as a whole or to the satisfaction of the world's many expectations. We have a commitment with ourselves, our own truth. With our happiness. It is only a consequence that happy people do live better together.

WORK

"I will not be 'famous,' 'great.' I will go on adventuring, changing, opening my mind and my eyes, refusing to be stamped and stereotyped. The thing is to free one's self: to let it find its dimensions, not be impeded."
–Virginia Woolf, diary

I got a job at an innovative small company that did an incredible job bringing senior business executives together to exchange knowledge and create more efficient, sustainable and better-performing corporations. It was founded and run by a visionary, my boss, a passionate entrepreneur who trusted me and my work. From the beginning, he gave me autonomy to work independently, establish priorities, create and implement projects and manage my own time. In a small company, I had the ability to make things happen without the usual obstacles of corporations' hierarchies and politics, and because I designed and proposed many of the projects we'd be working on myself, I spent a lot of time on tasks I actually quite enjoyed. I made enough money to live comfortably in London and save some.

Nevertheless, I felt unsatisfied with the professional path I was on. At times, I actually felt quite unhappy. I felt that working for a small organization, without a shiny brand on my resume would be damaging to my career, and that after dedicating so much to my development I deserved to be somewhere more prestigious. It bothered me when I had to explain where I worked and what I did, that the name and title didn't speak for themselves. I looked at people around me, friends, former classmates and others in my social circle, working at blue-chip corporations or renowned investment banks where they made huge sums of money, and felt sorry for myself. What had they done differently? What had I done wrong?

I started on a process of continuous, self-enforced dissatisfaction that eventually put me in a very unhappy place. I completely overlooked the positive aspects of my job and the many issues my friends seemed to face at theirs—exhaustingly long hours, the lack of autonomy in big corporations, being largely dedicated to uninteresting, boring tasks. Most importantly, I overlooked the fact that they were doing jobs I actually never cared for or wished I was doing. Instead, I only looked at everything I seemed to be missing. I chose to feel frustrated, unaccomplished and ashamed. I didn't stop to examine if I was missing anything *I actually wanted or needed.*

John Hunt was an organizational behavior professor and an authority on leadership. He believed companies assume that managing people is a science. They rely too much on establishing processes and structures, in logic, when what really inspires people to do more and better is entirely irrational, such as emotion and creativity. He argued, for instance, that when they are designing roles, recruiting and managing talent, employers put an enormous effort in outlining and finding the right competencies and skills, or what an individual should be able to do. However, as important as the ability is the motivation to do a job, what will be in it for those specific individuals. Just as relevant as looking at employee's skills is understanding how different work environments, reward systems and lifestyles will impact them. Quite often, lagging performance is due to a lack of motivation, not skill.

He created a framework to assess people's motivations, the things that drive us professionally and that bring us satisfaction while at work. Motivators include money, lifestyle, security, variety, affiliation with a team, recognition, power, autonomy and personal growth. The goal was to help companies manage and reward their people more effectively, conscious of what really drives them, and help individuals become more aware of what they want as they navigate through their careers. To help us become more conscious of the things that can bring each of us professional satisfaction, to avoid commonplaces, and ultimately feel happier at work.

Many of us will go through our entire careers without thinking properly about what we want from them, or how our work is helping us achieve what we want from life in general. We refer back to the collective hierarchy of values to go after the same rewards, the same goals, and then wonder why we don't feel satisfied. Going by without ever becoming aware that there are professional implications to our idiosyncratic human essence. And then we go on to punish ourselves for not being the frontrunner of a race we don't really care about running.

. . .

It is impossible to properly assess our satisfaction, to make career choices, and ultimately to thrive at our jobs unless we know what we are looking for ourselves. When I compared my job to my friends,' with resentment, the parameters that made me upset were certainly not picked by me. I actually quite enjoyed feeling empowered to make decisions and move on with my projects, far from the many layers of approval that are common in large corporations. I believed that the work my organization and I did was meaningful, that it mattered. And most importantly, I don't think I really cared about the big brand and status myself. While it would have been nice to make more money, I certainly didn't need it. I actually lived quite well. If I stepped out of everyone else's shoes and looked at things from my own perspective, based on my individual aspirations and my values, I was actually in quite a happy place. And while this may sound like the words of Pollyanna, in times of frustration I have learned that there is always something positive to be found in our work. Every job has its problems. But it is our own choice to make every day entirely about them.

A friend who works in the fine arts took me to Venice for the opening of the Art Biennale, perhaps the world's most important art exhibition, where virtually everyone in contemporary arts gathers every other year. And I was surprised to hear every single person I met and spoke to—dealers, curators, consultants—complain incessantly about the field. At first curious about their work, I eventually got tired of hearing their ongoing grumbling on how hard their lives were. Their exhaustion over big egos, how impossibly hard it was at the beginning, terrible pay, the industry's unstructured and inefficient practices. They complained while sipping champagne at the fancy Venice Bauer Hotel. And I thought to myself, astonished: these are people who work with art! They spend their days surrounded by creative expression. Even if their job is finance, brokering deals or insuring artwork, they still get to do so in a world of beauty. How could they not be inspired?

If anyone has been able to *choose* the field they work in, it has to be people who work in art. All of us others sort of fell into our places. And for that matter, their complaints are applicable to any other industry: egos, early-stage challenges, inefficiencies. While problems are an unavoidable reality of work, we all chose to highlight our individual misfortune, to hold tight to our misery, and to complain more and louder. We want our issues to be harder than others'. We must suffer more so that merely surviving behind that computer screen can become a source of pride. We chose to focus on what is not there. On what the others seem to have. Some people I know manage to brag and complain—about the same job. Those are habits of our times. We completely disregard things we might actually find pleasant, and most importantly whether, deep down, we are missing anything we care about at all.

When measuring myself up against others I also forgot, and I don't think I'm alone in doing that, about my own individual journey. I ignored how far I had come and the different circumstances that may have put someone else in their position, and me in mine. A foreigner, working in a second language, with few local ties and no network of connections. Young. But when we put ourselves up for comparison we don't wonder if the others came from far or near, if they had a guiding hand, if they've been on the road for longer. Every time I took a step forward in my career, I put aside where I had come from, to reset my standards for comparison. I would keep looking up, searching for an ever-more successful group of people to rebuild a sense of underachievement—disregarding my previous efforts and my own, individual future goals.

I never stopped to acknowledge the uniqueness of my path. I forgot that, growing up, I had never even heard of the jobs I came to admire, and perhaps unconsciously envy. How could I have been better prepared? How could I have known better? How could I have carefully planned each step towards the certainty of realization, without the support of ongoing guidance, a panoramic understanding of life's many choices? Without the confidence of those who know where they're headed, my resources limited to the values from my family and my own curiosity. Creating and grasping every opportunity for growth, but still bounded by my limited awareness of possibilities and of my own strength. By the random choices the world presented. Dancing with life, with some ability and grace, but only to the rhythms it chose to play to me. Professions, skillsets, lifestyle, money. We do the best we can with the hand we are dealt. How much would we have done differently, had we known it all? Had we had our eyes wide open, aware of every direction we could take? If all roads were smooth and clear and all the necessary tools were always at hand? There is no way to know.

But I can try to acknowledge that I did my best, proud of looking backwards at my own taken path, and forward, to walk with conviction to satisfy my own needs only. Or at least to one day find out what they might be.

Some people may well be intrinsically driven by money and prestige, and if so, that's what they should aim for in their professional lives. Money and prestige should be the basis for all of their career choices, and that is a good thing—for them. This is not an argument against any convention, but against their blind pursuit. Because of our personalities and the different contexts in which we all live—age, geography, culture, whether we have a family requiring time and financial support—we should want drastically different things from our careers. So it makes no sense to strive for the same rewards, to measure by the same standards. Careers, like individuals, are not comparable. Our unique and ever-changing motivations provide for a lifetime of thinking.

...

We are responsible for building our own identities. We have our intrinsic traits and we are born into a context, but within those parameters, it is ultimately up to us to define who we are. In literature, characters in a story can be flat or round. A flat character in a novel, for example, is one-dimensional, strightforward, clearly established and easy to understand. It has few characteristics and doesn't change. It's just mean, like a cold-blooded villain. Or sweet, like a young lady in love. Round characters are multi-faceted. Their personalities are nuanced and complex, and they present new traits as the story unfolds. They change. How we perceive their characteristics changes as we learn of their distinct motivations, making it harder to judge their behavior. All human beings in real life, of course, are round. We are many things, we are many. We are professionals, citizens, explorers, lovers, parents, activists, friends. Because we all must play multiple roles, it is ultimately up to us to assign weight to them, to determine which of them matter. Which roles will stand out to constitute the person we look at in the mirror and project out to the world.

A friend of mine, an artist, was visiting London and invited me to a party with his friends. I arrived at a warehouse in the outskirts of the city and saw a very edgy crowd. His friends were effortlessly hip, unpretentious and had a kind of rugged, rebellious energy. Everyone wore black and the music was, in itself, an experience. We chatted and danced until I got curious. I couldn't exactly place any of those people in my repertoire of common professions—I couldn't tell what they did, so I asked my friend. He was slightly puzzled with my question, as if he thought I wasn't enjoying something, and almost surprised, he asked back: "Why does it matter?"

I then realized I had been talking to those people for a couple of hours and no one asked me what I did for a living. In my day-to-day life, people will ask about your job before you finish stating your name. It is a crucial part of our understanding of another person; there's an established place in someone's identity it should occupy.

At that party, that place wasn't there. It was filled with their rough confidence, with their laughter, with their leather boots and invariably black outfits, the music. That night was fun, and a beautiful lesson for someone in the corporate life.

Sometimes I still remind myself of it when I catch myself wondering, judgmentally: what does someone do?

—Does it really matter?

Becoming conscious of the answer enables us to structure our lives with things in their right place, to allocate our time and energy and connect with the sides of ourselves that matter to us. Society, of course, sets its standards—and it's so easy to blindly take them for granted. No matter which context you're in, there will be an assigned importance to work and career, greater or smaller. We don't have to follow. We have every right, in fact we must determine the role we want work to play in our lives. Only then can it be fulfilling.

Some will find that their professions are a strong aspect of their identity. Their job is a lot of who they are. It provides them with a purpose in life, it directs their social relationships, it helps constitute the people they want to be. Not so much for others. Others may want work to be a place where they make money: either just enough to live comfortably or a whole lot more. We may want to satisfy our passion, to fulfill our creative urge, to feel connected to the world, to give. Some just need to fill their days! So even before we think about whether *a* job is speaking to our inner self, before thinking of motivations per se, we must become aware of what should be the role of *any* job in our lives. What does it mean, for you, to work?

. . .

My generation cemented this belief that work should be synonymous with personal fulfilment. That we must never settle for anything that isn't in perfect alignment with our interests and values and must ultimately find ourselves at our jobs. While I think the principle is noble and certainly worth pursuing for many, my issue with unrestricted generalization remains: do all of us really want that? Maybe some just want to pay the bills and go find themselves hiking, taking care of their children, doing origami. Aren't those just as noble?

But now, purpose is the norm. Purpose is what we should pursue. And once again, we might find ourselves unhappy, filled with dissatisfaction, missing something from our work life that it was never meant to provide in the first place. Meanwhile, the world is full of purpose to be found elsewhere.

There was a time I felt extremely passionate about my job, proud of it. I worked really closely with my clients and felt I genuinely helped them think through and overcome their challenges. At presentations I used to see satisfaction in their eyes, comfort that we understood their businesses. When they called and I picked up the phone I could hear comfort and relief that we were there for them at very challenging times. Those sighs of relief meant everything for me. I thought my work mattered and it fulfilled me. I grew. But my role went through a revamp and transformed entirely. With the changes, suddenly everything was different. There was a new front-line team dealing with clients, and I now managed projects in a different structure, internally. I hated it.

The new responsibilities didn't provide me with the same sense of purpose or excitement. I didn't think the work was as relevant or impactful, and suddenly I was extremely unhappy. Where my job used to make me a satisfied human being, now I felt left with a hole. More than just being in touch with clients, I missed having my eyes and ears out to the world. It kept me connected, excited. And I felt I just couldn't deliver without being close to the issues we were working on, immersed entirely in the context and able to spot solutions and opportunities at any time. But there was no way out of it—the restructuring was across the entire company and that was how we were going to operate moving forward.

This happened when, for a number of reasons, it wasn't the right time to change jobs, so I felt stuck and miserable. My dissatisfaction spilled over into every aspect of my life.

Wishing work didn't matter so much to me, I started thinking about friends who didn't talk much about their jobs, who didn't seem to really bother. They seemed to be living for something else. Whether in less-than-thrilling roles due to circumstances, too busy with things they cared about more, or just bored, they didn't feel an existential threat because their job wasn't something about which they were absolutely passionate. I noticed they were finding joy outside the office. And perhaps it was time for me to change my paradigm.

Maybe work was just a place where I went daily, did something as well as I could, got paid for it, and moved to a position that would enable me to go do something else. Simple as that. And I stayed for as long as it was necessary, never thrilled, but peaceful, and satisfied outside of work.

We can still control our identities, no matter how the world might want to see us. Gisele Bundchen is perhaps the greatest of all Brazilian supermodels. She stunned the reporter at an interview when she said, very naturally, that she is not "a fashion person." "Modelling is my job, it's not who I am," she explained.

Actively deciding that her work does not define her, she puts aside what she may represent for others and all external expectations to embrace what she represents to herself. The article elaborated: she also happens to be an extremely successful business woman, a wife, a mother. A dedicated, skilled yogi, a passionate environmentalist. She is what she wants to be—and that's not a model. That's just her job. And the reporter understood, and wrote in his headline: "Gisele Bundchen Is a Force of Nature."

Of course, circumstances at our jobs, as in life overall, can be very different from what we expect. At times work will fail to play its role in our complex identities, not delivering on whatever we need or hope from it, whether that's finding ourselves or just making cash. In any case, **the great thing about becoming more aware of ourselves is realizing that we can *change* ourselves.** If we are conscious of a genuine shortfall in our career, of what we expected it would do for our wellbeing, we can try to find it in other aspects of our lives. We can try to appreciate some other advantage the current job may provide. We can decide it's time for a move. We are in control.

Being aware of our priorities means being able to consciously change them. Our individual motivations, our own lives, our power to shape them.

. . .

In the context I live in, professional success is probably the metric most commonly used to assess a human being. Luckily, that isn't the case everywhere. It is inadequate by its nature. Let's play a game and ignore for the moment that each individual lives for something different; that everyone has their own intimate determinants of happiness. Let's assume it makes sense to measure everyone on the same standard: success. Let's take success as a value for all, the ultimate determinant of human worth: it is what we should pursue, dream of and envy. To uphold that premise we would first need to define success. Does it mean outperforming peers and growing faster in a career? Does it mean changing titles, Manager, Director, Head of, VP? Is it impeccable delivery, exceeding expectations, in time? Having an impact? For whom? If success is how we determine the worth of people, what universal standard will we measure them against?

The assistant of a former boss of mine had been a personal assistant for over thirty years. She was extremely dedicated, aware of everything gravitating in our boss's orbit. Each detail of his past and future schedule, what was, wasn't, and would become a priority—she anticipated his needs and had everything in place before he even asked. Sometimes I thought she read his thoughts. She loved her job. We became closer than colleagues, true friends. I was young and living in a new city, and in a way, she felt like a mom. I admired and looked up to her work deeply, and thought of her as the definition of commitment and success.

A director at the first company I worked for resigned unexpectedly for a role at a competitor. I had only worked with her very little, but enough to learn that she was smart and dedicated. She was a tall German woman who spoke in a measured, low tone of voice because she knew people would stop and listen. And they did. Sharp yet polite, elegant and approachable, she was admired effortlessly. Everyone knew her, or of her, and people were unhappy with her departure, some because they liked working with her or for her, others because they knew she'd been doing great things at our main rival.

At the end of her last day it surprised me to see her walking through the office, stopping by every single desk to say goodbye, and giving people hugs. She started with those more distant and made her way across every department. Her bosses, IT support, everyone. She had been there for a long time and we were small enough to have a feeling of community in our work environment. Things got slightly emotional when she finally made it to her own team, giving long, heartfelt hugs and goodbyes, and she finished by her desk, where she picked up her stuff to leave. And suddenly, spontaneously, everyone—everyone—stood up, gathered and started applauding as she moved from her desk and made her way out of the office. She walked down rows and rows of desks through our open-plan office and left with a standing ovation from over 100 people,

people with whom she worked very closely, some who only knew her by name. Her resented boss, cleaning staff, everyone applauded until she had left. That, I thought, and nothing else, must be success.

Straight out of university, young bankers and lawyers get into an exhausting routine of long and intense working hours in highly-stressful environments. They will spend most of their twenties, and probably a considerable part of their thirties with handsome pay checks and little time to spend them. Many plan to work hard enough for ten or twenty years and then either retire or move into something less demanding and more pleasant, having built the financial structure to live comfortably. I used to think their approach was madness. Fond of my own youthful adventures and long nights of sleep, I couldn't see the logic in spending your most vivid years, your most precious time, locked in an office tower. To stop working while still fully capable, only less curious, less adventurous, and more tired.

Of course, I never recognized that the strategy doesn't fit into *my* logic. It doesn't play well with my tastes, my perspective and my attachment to youth. That there is no such thing as most precious time; all time is equally precious. And if they dedicate their youth to their future wealth, and do so because it suits their taste, the life they dream of—whether for the money, the stability or even for the status, if that's what they so intimately crave—

extra hours are a small price to pay for a lifetime of idiosyncratic success and expensive happiness.

As everything in life, success is defined within. Firstly, whether it matters at all, and secondly, what it entails. We risk spending our lives running after a loosely-defined concept, a poorly-established convention that means absolutely nothing in itself. That says nothing about who we are, our intellectual capacity, our skills or competence, and by no means can it account for anyone's value as a human being. An illusion. And we cannot, we must not, chase something that we don't care about, something we can't even really define.

. . .

Money is great. It provides for our most basic needs, and more. It gives comfort, stability, courage and pleasure, there is no denying. However, it does not account for talent, vision, entitlement, certainly not for taste and, for that matter, for professional success. Unlike success, money is indeed well-defined and quantifiable, but that definitely doesn't mean it can measure achievement or determine happiness. Examples are everywhere.

There are so many, strong social constructs associated with having money that a lot of our pursuit is completely unrelated from the actual delights it can buy. It feels like we are mostly chasing the associations—status, respect, belonging. We think of money not as a means of exchange—even for the most extravagant idiosyncrasies—but as a credential that will open the doors to a better, a more glamorous, to the right side of life. Having it becomes perhaps less important than *being perceived to have it.*

In his 2007 book, *Consuming Life*, Polish philosopher Zygmunt Bauman defines our contemporary world as the society of consumption. He describes how individuals in this society believe happiness lies in wanting and getting, the satisfaction of fulfilling our continuous desires, in achieving gratification. If we are just able to fulfill that wish, that longing, then we will be happy. But the promise is never met. Never before in humanity, Bauman claims, has happiness been made so trivial. In the society of consumption, the promise of happiness is constantly reinforced, and never delivered on. The vacuum it leaves is simply filled with our next desire.

I observe some people who I think are quite unhappy with the unspoken convention that keeps our financial affairs private, not openly discussing exactly how much money we make or have accumulated. Of course, if we are chasing after a value that isn't our own, if it is the world that determined that money matters, and how much it matters, only the world can validate the greatness of our achievement. Making or having money must become part of our identity. And we consume, and associate with a lifestyle, with brands, with places that will assure that the beauty of our finances doesn't go unnoticed. Only the world out there can assure us that we are happy. We made it!

The cult of money, however, isn't a novelty of our times. In the 16th century, Calvinist Protestants believed that people were born destined to salvation, or not. They looked for signs of that predestination, and that included the ability to make money and accumulate wealth. Calvinists would work hard to be able to assure themselves and show the world that they were amongst the chosen ones, destined to end in paradise. Five centuries later, many of us, believers and atheists, still seem to think that money, for itself, has the power to save us.

. . .

The logics of business became so rooted in our society that we started incorporating principles and practices of corporations into our lives, leading them as if they were businesses.

Take the notion of failure, for example. It's a perfectly human phenomenon: trying something and failing, or achieving a flawed result, not doing something quite perfectly. Failing. Since we are children: we fall from bikes or we can't get our heads around math. We then fail to impress the boys and girls we like, try and fail our driving test, fail at cooking a special dinner. We fail with the people we love, fail on our New Year's resolutions, fail to fall asleep, and we inevitably fail at work. We make mistakes. Being unsuccessful is an unavoidable, frequent, and important part of the human experience.

But businesses will do everything to avoid failure. Business needs precision. Business needs efficiency. Predictability. Even though it is fundamentally against our flawed human nature, we try to implement the same principle in our lives. We are uncomfortable with mistakes. We punish for failure, both ourselves and our children and, and we strive to operate less like humans, and more like machines screwing in wheels on new cars. Looking for perfection in invariably imperfect beings is an obvious, but recurrent recipe for stress and frustration.

From when I started working in the corporate world, the idea of 'growth' has always bothered me. I used to come across analyses on companies' earnings, and next to massive revenues and profits, there were complaints about and disappointment with the growth. Grew too little. Future challenges for growth. Corporations the size of a country's economy, double digit profit margins, but disappointing their investors because of their limited prospects for growth...! It was slightly naive, but inevitable, to think, "Why do they need to grow? Don't they look big and healthy enough?"

What about people? We are now obsessed with growth. With getting better. Being a better professional, a better citizen, a better parent. Earning more, reading more, meditating for longer. We let go of the natural course of our development, we cannot feel satisfaction. Always ignoring the greatness of our current state of being for growth. Never good enough. Is there a basis for that need? Or is the need for growth just a symptom of chronic human dissatisfaction?

. . .

One day, just recently, I realized that I had no idea of what I wanted to do with my life. I knew of many things I didn't want, I can think of a few things I like, even am passionate about, a few dreams sketched all over the place. But no clear connection with a profession, with a type of job I could find on listings, and much less a structured plan on how to find the right place to be in the future. Life and my own choices took me to a good place, but when I looked ahead, I couldn't see where the road was leading. It was scary. We learn that building a career, that becoming someone in life requires planning, but how do you plan for undetermined goals?

I discussed it with a friend. I'm thirty and I don't know what I want to do. He didn't think it mattered much: a lot of people don't. And I decided to run some informal research and reached out to people who I perceived as being focused, well-established on their path, all around my age, to ask if they remembered when they became sure of what they wanted from their careers. If they had a sudden epiphany, if their path had always been clear. And I was surprised with their responses: nobody was really all that sure, still. A few were actually quite lost, despite their seemingly cohesive career.

A high school classmate whose father was an engineer, always wanted to be an engineer, loved engineering school, has a great job as an engineer and teaches engineering told me: "I have no idea of what I want to do." She didn't resent it, she said it with a joyful curiosity, like a young girl who had been putting on a clever trick for the past 30 years. Another former classmate, now a researcher doing a PhD program at one of the best universities in the world confessed, "I don't know what I'm doing, where I'm going. I'm so unsure. I have so many questions."

Betraying my disdain for comparisons, I felt quite relieved hearing about other people's uncertainty. My friend was right, a lot of people don't know. Maybe most people don't know. Many of us will probably die without being sure. But we move forward, experimenting, testing, dreaming, and working hard. There is an excitement to the openness, there is so much we wouldn't try if we had always known the answer. And I am coming to believe that if you're truthful to yourself, if you're aware of what moves you, just vaguely conscious of how you want to live, if you let go of expectations built somewhere other than your heart, the search in itself may be worth the ride.

LOOK

It is widely known that Brazilians are obsessed with aesthetics. We are a nation built of miscegenation, with a culture whose value lies—or rather dances—in the plurality of its origins. Yet, disturbingly, our surroundings strictly dictate what our body, skin, hair, clothes and smile should look like. We are all hostages of these passively accepted aesthetic standards and establish sad, self-confining social circles—echo chambers that constantly reinforce their own reductive, boring styles. Deviating from the mainstream look-and-feel comes with an unavoidable set of assumptions, judgment, and unsettledness in affiliations with social groups.

Brazil accounts for almost 10% of the beauty industry's global sales. As soon as their permanent teeth come through, virtually every single child, regardless of the seriousness of their need or economic background, gets braces. I estimate that around half of my friends have had work done on their noses. At least 80% of my girlfriends have had some type of plastic surgery on their breasts: added to, taken off, or both (one of them four times, and she claims she is still not fully satisfied: "he hasn't managed to get my nipples fully aligned"). All of my 30-something friends are starting to fill their first signs of ageing with Botox. The word "vaidade," vanity in Portuguese, doesn't have the negative conception of self-absorption and conceit of its English translation; it is rather a valued attribute, with a more nuanced connotation, alluding to taking good care of oneself and maintaining a polished appearance.

. . .

The gay community is also heavily driven by aesthetics, imposing high, rigorous appearance standards to those who want to fit in. Having gone through the same struggles growing up, still facing the same inclusion challenges and being victims of the same stigmas, it would seem logical that gay people would build a community of understanding and mutual support. But no. We are terribly judgmental. Remarkably so when it comes to the body. Gay men are obsessed with an ideal look established for our own (and others') bodies, and more than any other group, we strive to bring our physique to the core of our identity. The cult of the body is a self-enforcing belief within our social group; fitness is desired because it's been established that it matters, and it matters because it's desired.

Some say it started because gay men, for long deprived of marriage aspirations and the comfort of monogamy, were "on the market" more consistently, and for longer. Having to rely on their appearance constantly, they were never able to afford to let things slip. The body is an instrument for validation and sexual satisfaction. Others argue that, going through a lifetime of being a misfit and living on the margins, gay men develop an inner need to be perfect—and most importantly, to prove our masculinity in a men's world. Through muscles. To distance ourselves from any trace of femininity that may be related to being gay. The body becomes an instrument for social acceptance, tamed by the values of our patriarchal society.

Now imagine what growing up gay, in Brazil, does to your perception of yourself. When I was a kid, my family jokingly called me "fornalha," Portuguese for those large industrial iron-smelting furnaces—devices they claimed were similar to my nose in scale. I was then an awkward-looking teenager—always on the shorter range of the spectrum, terrible skin, wild hair I could never really sort out, and braces.

Approaching my 20s, things became a little better, but I was still unremarkable. I was still short, helplessly thin, and it is known that cartilage, and thus noses, never stop growing. I tried weightlifting to build up my body, without much success. Very fast metabolism. Always surrounded with beautiful friends, in beautiful social circles, I had to learn to establish my place through other means, and deal with my lack of confidence in my appearance. Eventually, I made peace with it, for most of the time. But it didn't last for very long.

One day, grown up and past the aesthetic agony of the teens, looking better groomed and feeling less concerned, I was at the beach with a friend when we met another friend of his. This was a guy who had the so-called "perfect body." A god. He was tall, tanned, toned and lean, I could see the grooves between the muscles in his arms and the well-defined v-line below his tight abs shining under the sun. And I noticed how, in his presence, I could barely speak, but not because I felt attracted. I felt ashamed.

Simply being around that guy made me feel uncomfortable. Today I can't really tell if he made me feel irrelevant, invisible, or if it made me wish I was. I no longer remember the guy's name, but that encounter had an enormous impact on me.

Maybe I happened to be in a particularly insecure state of spirit. It's hard to tell what happened inside my head on that day. Being faced with that guy's fitness—both physical, the one everyone could see, and cultural, the body securing his position at the top of our value hierarchy—shook my confidence to its core. I went home shortly after, taking with me a lifetime of renewed insecurities, and that experience changed my relationship with my body forever.

I now see it as a reminder of how fragile our belief in ourselves is, in a world ruled by conventions and standards. On that day, the very common habit of comparing made me feel unattractive, uninteresting, unworthy. It surfaced what I believed was my complete irrelevance in a world of perfect looks.

At that time I used to exercise, more for the habit than for any body goals, and I ate normally, often more concerned with convenience than with nutrition. I was normal. But I came back from that beach feeling completely abnormal: for days I felt disgusting, barely able to look at myself. The body was average—there is no better way to describe it. But it felt disgusting. It felt like a revelation: all my romantic insuccesses, all of the less-than-perfect sexual experiences I had previously blamed myself over, years of lacking confidence, my mediocrity as a gay man. Everything so clearly explained—with this body, what else could you expect?

And it became clear that I had to change. After a whole life cultivating my Capricornian discipline, it actually felt quite natural to start exercising twice a day, six times a week. I followed diets with the rigor of a dedicated army soldier, invariably slept the recommended number of hours, drank three liters of water daily. I stopped drinking alcohol and eating sugar, anything fried or processed, gluten, dairy, salt. I started studying and understanding the functioning mechanism of the body like an amateur bodybuilder, then applied my learnings to an ever-stricter set of rules, which I followed uncompromisingly. I started on a journey that, while transforming my lifestyle and the shape of my body, warped my perception of myself and completely unsettled the balance of my mind.

I shed almost half of the fat in my body and gained the same weight back in muscle. As my body changed, my goals changed too, becoming bolder, more rigorous, and moving closer to that unachievable illusion of perfection. I looked up to stronger models and realized my physical potential at the expense of my satisfaction with myself. That year my old body went, but so much damage was left. Instead of feeling proud and confident, I was increasingly distressed, anxious and disappointed.

At that stage, I felt worse than fat: I thought I was skinny-fat. Bone, skin, and fat. And the healthy habits that had been signs of discipline and determination became an obsession, part of a condition that started to dictate my routine and social life. They occupied all of my headspace and irreparably messed with my peace of mind. I lived for my body. Not *my* body: that other body, the body I didn't have. The one I feared I'd never have.

My distorted perspective on reality and the ever-stretching objectives turned my mindset of drive and transformation into an endless loop of frustration and self-deprecation. Eating before attending dinners. Religiously exercising in the morning and the evening. Dragging myself to the gym after long, 12-hour workdays. Suppressing all of my perception of taste. Decreasing contact with friends, who mostly gather to celebrate, either eat, drink, or both. Eating way too much, fasting. Cooking and carrying food everywhere—including when I travelled to visit my parents. And guilt, guilt, guilt, for not doing more, for not working harder, for not being there.

One day I visited a sports-performance doctor, who ran yet another measure of my body fat percentage: 8%, well below the male average. The doctor told me it was possible to reach 5% without compromising my body functions, and I went on the impossible mission of getting rid of the extra through more diet adjustments, more rigor, less contact with the world outside. My parameters were no longer healthy or beautiful, it was maintaining minimal vital functions. Today, I look at pictures of that time and I have absolutely no recollection of ever having that body. I never once saw it in the mirror.

It took professional help for me to understand that no objective could possibly be that extreme. But most importantly, that achieving a determined shape was not the primary reason for my existence, that there isn't an image I had to live to pursue. That an ideal body does not exist. To understand that my body belongs to me, and not the opposite. That it was beautiful—that it had always been beautiful, in its way. That the standards and the models are external, they are irrelevant, they are absurd. They are nothing.

Aesthetic projections can unconsciously take over our lives and become not an inspiration, not even an ideal, but a set of conditional parameters for living. Our bodies should be the manifestation of our individuality to the world. They are our only instrument for interaction and experimentation, our home. If we are not careful, they end up escaping from the control of our subjectivity and deep intimacy, they are no longer reflections of our inner-selves. They grow distant from our essence, enslaved by our minds to tirelessly pursue the collective idea of beauty.

. . .

The cult of the body is arbitrary, irrational and cruel. The notion that there is such thing as a determined type of physique we should all either have, or strive to have is absurd! We are all born different and have different motivations. This idea leads to a very unhappy life, at the very least. The evolving concept of *a* perfect body travels through the minds and lives of people across cultures, determining what we should look up to, work towards, or feel guilty about. Interestingly, it isn't substantiated by any objective benefit or pleasure related to having a determined shape. For most of us, the idea of fitness has been doing more harm than good.

Consider our bias and individual struggles against fat (and the consequent, ruthless discrimination of fat people). What is it based on? Where does it come from? A health-conscious mentality, one could argue. But interestingly, while there is no doubt that being obese carries serious risks and is responsible for thousands of deaths every year, there is no scientific consensus that being simply overweight is unhealthy at all. Studies have shown that being "overweight," but not obese, does not increase an individual's risk of death—some associating a slightly higher BMI with a lower risk of dying, on average.

Fat is not necessarily bad. On the other hand, what have been well documented by doctors and psychologists, are the increasing rates and devastating effects of eating disorders and body dysmorphia—those directly related to the idea that being fat is somehow negative. While I lack the medical expertise, I think it's safe to say that being somewhat over or underweight doesn't necessarily make anyone unhealthy. Certainly not in comparison with a dangerous alternative: perfect bodies, built in association with a severe impact on an individual's mental health.

But that's not much of a secret: we all know that for most, fitness goals derive from the (artificial) concept of the attractive, the sexy, and not a concern with health and longevity. The pursuit of a perfect body is almost always a product of minds that can't escape the norms dictated by society. The health argument is, today, either a sales pitch for the fitness industry, or a coy lie we use to add some grace to our otherwise vain, sad body obsessions. Again, for as long as we rely on collective standards, we are trapped. Alienated from our own drivers of wellbeing, we are either guilty for not conforming with the standard or frustrated with the emptiness of our achievements.

Another non-scientific obviousness: a fit body, whether lean or muscled, has absolutely no correlation to superior sexual performance. It's not a matter of endurance. It's more of an art, and certainly not a race. Anyone who experiments with both fit and unfit, just a few times, will be able to confirm—and everyone should try. And if those with so-called "hot" bodies do not have better sex, they can only seem superiorly attractive due to cemented external concepts of beautiful and sexy, never due to relevant, empirical experience. We are not, instinctively, more turned on by fit bodies than others—simply because the definition of sexy doesn't come wired in our brains. It's a construct!

What we do feel, of course, is the pressure to adjust our desires to common sense, and a fear of being seen as a freak, due to which many end up hiding and suppressing what may be their true, unconventional sex drivers. These cemented, fabricated desires for what we call sexy don't indicate that you'll ever feel any more pleasure—but the opposite. Objectively: a fit, "perfect" body is in no way better than a "normal," an "overweight," or a "too skinny" body. And ultimately, freaks simply have a lot more fun.

When I see a "perfect" body today, one like the guy at the beach, my delicate psyche sways between two feelings. There is my instinctive self-deprecation, envy, because you can't run away from the haunting pressure of social standards so easily. And there is compassion. I am conscious of the life-consuming efforts required to get there; more aware of the restrictive, self-consuming mind-space that lifestyle may have led to.

Unrealistic body standards are the cause of anxiety and depression in many, or at the very least, get in the way of having fun, of being ourselves and enjoying the human experience to the fullest. They are the source of constant guilt for many. And they're not going away unless we actively choose to set them aside. Not by simply rebelling against healthy food or exercise, but, again, connecting with our inner-selves and individual aspirations. And chasing our own goals! Bodybuilders, for instance, dedicate to shaping their body, gaining muscle mass and losing body fat as a deliberate choice. It is not an unconscious effort to comply with the norms of beauty or to assert their worth as individuals. That is fine. It is great; to find something of genuine interest and pursue it. But we must understand our motivations, we must pursue goals that come from within. And balance life accordingly, never moving forward blindly or depriving ourselves from anything we truly love—whether friends, CrossFit or KFC.

And we must let go of judgment, of ourselves and others, providing space for us all to just be. I heard a friend of mine, late 30s, gay, smart and handsome, elaborate articulately over his complex gym/body strategy: you have to go enough so your body looks hot and attractive. But you can't go too much, because if you look too ripped people will think you're a gym rat (shallow). And they will see you at the gym too often, they might think you don't have a life. You have to assess your body and recent attendance and decide strategically whether to go. So basically, working hard was no longer enough either—one needs a *strategy*. I laughed at our helpless captive condition in this world, how our every move is dictated by how we may be perceived. The mental shackles of contemporary free humans.

There is, of course, a case for keeping healthy. There is a case for having a certain lifestyle. For the pleasures of endorphins. There is a strong case about genuinely feeling well within your body—whatever it may look like—and our amazing ability to transform it, which we can indeed exercise. But we must separate habits that can be fulfilling from baseless, external aesthetic pressures. The line is easy to spot; unlike our internal push for sweat and change, the obsessive pursuit of a body image does not give one pleasure. It's unrealistic. It's never ending. And it may take way too much time to realize that a "perfect" body cannot be a source of fulfilment or happiness.

. . .

What is beauty? What does it mean to be beautiful? To "look good?" There is a scientific understanding that suggests some physical features are indeed aesthetically pleasing to all humans: regular, straight features, a symmetrical face, a well-distributed body. Research claims that perceiving beauty is an evolutionary tool, an instinct; uniform characteristics could indicate a better genotype, more appropriate for procreation. Anomalies, asymmetries, disproportion would all be signs of relatively poorer health and genetic fitness.

However, humans are a lot more complex than peacocks that compare their fanned-out feathers, and our current understanding of beauty is cultural, not biological. Both individual and collective parameters and processes get in the way of our pure, evolutionary response. Our own individual preferences, desires, fetishes. And conditioning from our families, the media, our social circle.

Umberto Eco, the philosopher, did a thorough study of the changing concept of beauty through history, published in his book, *On Beauty: A History of a Western Idea*. Through representations of "the beautiful" in art, he presents multiple, evolving "aesthetic ideals" and how they came to be in different societies through time. From the ancient Greeks, through the Middle Ages, the Renaissance, until more current, mass-media times.

After looking at how the meaning of beauty transformed across the centuries, his conclusion was obvious: "Beauty has never been absolute and immutable but has taken on different aspects depending on the historical period and the country."

The very definition of beauty, *that which pleases the senses*—the sight, specifically—accounts for its subjective nature. Beautiful can only come to be when it's before someone's senses, in front of someone's eyes. An observer must be pleased—beauty is conditional on the appreciation of another individual. The beautiful unseen, in itself, does not exist. The agent, the determinant of beauty, is the observer, not the object; it is us.

It is up to each of us to define beauty, claim it and embrace it, as you can't, objectively, *be* beautiful. You can only *feel* beautiful, please your own eyes when you look at yourself. **Beauty is a subjective experience—inside and out.**

Still, the concept is also associated with attraction, and influences our ability to connect with other people socially, sexually and romantically. Beautiful is interesting. One could argue that the collectively-established notion of beauty does matter, that there is an objective benefit from looking a certain way. Beautiful is attractive. Is that really the case, though? Does that attraction really mean anything?

Thinking of all the people I know, I see no correlation between conventional beauty and individuals that are more fulfilled sexually or romantically. I know many people, in fact, who, more or less in accordance with the standards, find themselves trapped in a world of vanity, narcissism and insecurity, dedicating so much energy to their appearance while never truly feeling satisfied.

If beautiful people do not feel happier, if they're not building more numerous and more meaningful connections, it is inevitable to wonder whether they really are more attractive in the first place. Maybe undeniable beauty doesn't last long enough to have any real-life impact. When we feel attraction, or claim we feel attraction, to that established standard of people, are we acknowledging a clear fact or reinforcing a stereotype?

Do we claim we like the undeniably beautiful because we feel truly, intimately attracted, or do we think we feel attracted because everyone claims to like them? Because the world has labeled them: ATTRACTIVE? The guidelines of social standards are so deeply rooted in our perception of the world, in our eyes and our minds. They are hardly distinguishable from our own instincts, from our primal, most animal desire to mate. What do we *really* like, if we were to think by ourselves alone?

Here is the outer world, again, controlling something at the heart of our individuality: our desire. Jumping ahead of ourselves and dictating what we should be attracted to, the meaning of beauty, what should and what shouldn't be an object for longing. It seems unlikely that those currently perceived as beautiful really do drive unanimous magnetism. Rationally, they can't possibly turn the entire world on—a simple absolute majority seems unlikely. But we think they do. And that we should certainly be turned on as well.

The controlling dynamics of the "collectively beautiful" and "individually attractive" are not only self-enforcing, they also have the expensive support of the beauty industry, celebrities and the media, the triumvirate of our aesthetic dictatorship. The owners and controllers of all beauty. The standards are so rooted in our daily life that we can't tell them from our own turn ons, and that trap is so hard to escape.

What if we were to rebel against all established notions, strip ourselves of preconceptions and wholeheartedly look for beauty in everyone—absolutely everyone—that we see, starting with ourselves? Is it really that unrealistic to claim we'd find it? To assume that, free from judgment, we'd be open to a richer aesthetic experience and, in different ways, attracted to all shapes and forms? Could we lust and love just anyone? Including ourselves? What a beautiful world that would be.

Life is more interesting if we learn to experience it by ourselves, with our own eyes and hands, not those who came before us. It has endless possibilities. It's within our power to redefine the meaning of beautiful, attractive. Or the opposite—encourage our curiosity and our aesthetic interest in the unconventional, the ugly. It's not just a word play: it's resignifying the world, this time from our own perspective. In a later anthology, *On Ugliness*, Umberto Ecco noted: "Ugliness is unpredictable and offers an infinite range of possibilities. Beauty is finite. Ugliness is infinite, like God."

. . .

The passage of time, and how it will keep scarring my face and my body, terrify me. They terrify many of us. We don't want to age, to seem to be ageing, to be reminded that we are ageing. Of course, all human beings understand, unconsciously, that ageing means getting closer to death. That going through days and years is, inevitably, walking towards our own individual extinction, at least on this plane, if not everywhere.

I don't think that's morbid or dramatic. It's a clear-cut fact, and one that we all get, if not rationally, at least within. So our fear of ageing is, ultimately, a fear of ending. It's instinctive. It seems somewhat natural. And the wrinkles, thinner and gray hair, flabby skin and hanging parts are constant reminders that there is no way around it, regardless of our Sisyphean efforts to try to hide them.

Aversion to ageing may seem understandable. But rationally, the loathing and our remedies against the aesthetic consequences of the passage of time, of course, are pointless: it will keep passing by, and we will all terminate, period. Psychologically, our efforts to look younger and fresher may still ease the pain imposed by the inevitability of death. Even so, I still advocate that we should be fully aware of the condition of our existence, connected with ourselves at every age, whether we choose to fight time, or not.

Our individual fears are certainly reinforced by an external world that obsesses with youth, appearance and consumption. It turns our honest concerns into a full denial of our natural path as humans, into non-conformism and, again, sadness. We cut ourselves no slack. The pressure to keep young turns the anesthetic illusion of stretching time, and any joy that may come with it, into a losing battle against the unavoidable. The disconnection with our natural evolution, to chase yet another social construct.

My mother used to say she wanted to die young, so she wouldn't have to grow old. I don't really think she meant it. Now close to 60, she takes care of her looks diligently, both day-to-day, and with a few occasional major interventions. Looking at our family pictures, people ask if she's my sister. She certainly feels the weight of time but seems to go through it in peace. She has fun. She eats consciously, but drinks as much as she feels like. She puts on gym clothes, but just to go through her daily errands, walking around in running shoes without ever running a single kilometer. Works eighty hours a week but stops for massage and applies Botox. Unapologetic and living fully. As her son, I don't want to believe she's ageing either, but she honestly seems to be doing great.

If we chose to embrace the palliative concealers of ageing, either for some unconscious peace of mind, or just because we like a certain look, I do think we should start doing so with more grace. Accepting our bodies' transformations, even if to fight against them. Embracing having lived longer and the evolving beauty of the human figure. Accepting that youth is a brief event, not a human state of being, and thinking of it as a pretty phase, not a die-hard goal. And always, always giving ourselves permission.

There is no predetermined clothing, hair, or lifestyle appropriate for people over 40, 50, 60. There are only choices, what we decide looks appropriate on us! Ageing is not an exercise in transforming to fit in, catching up with what becomes the new adequate. It is simply transforming, period. And gaining the courage to allow our hearts to speak out. The other day I saw an elderly lady dancing happily at a techno rave party. She must have been over 70. I can't remember ever observing a more liberating scene: her confidence in belonging, the freedom of her body and soul, her seeming control over her own state of being. When she was 63, Simone de Beavoir said, "time has stopped for me." She saw herself "installed in old age," even though she didn't feel old, her body not showing the slightest sign of declining health. The only thing that concerned her was her relationship with the future, and not being able to commit to anything for the long term: "I wouldn't dare saying 'in 30 years, in 40 years.' I feel my finitude." We all inevitably do.

From the opposite perspective, the aesthetics of maturity have always mesmerized me. The look of a fully blossomed figure, ripe, ready, but still bravely refusing to accept that it peaked. It's so easy to be beautiful when you're young. You just are. Beautiful by just *being*. Now, undergoing the beatings of time, growing old and *staying* beautiful, incorporating the body's changes with elegance and pride, that is for few. It carries a certain aesthetic weight: an individual who's been there. And makes it noticeable. Accepting time has its undeniable charm. It's an act of bravery, being fearless and confident over the power of your presence, still standing, restless, after all the years.

I don't think that will be me. I sort of stopped keeping track of my years already, surprised with how fast I was counting them up. Appreciating age on others is easy, the challenge is making peace with its pace for ourselves. And understanding where our own concerns with time end, and the many aesthetic norms start. I don't feel hopeless; with time, I think I may learn. I will have to. Luckily, the years bring you more than just bad joints and dry skin. In 1932, at the age of 50, Virginia Woolf wrote in her diary: "I do not believe in ageing, I believe in forever altering one's image to the sun. Hence my optimism."

. . .

One could argue that I can't even begin to describe the devastating effects of pursuing collective standards of beauty on people's lives and in our society, not having experienced any of them as a women. They would be right. Women's looks have been and are assessed, scrutinized, judged, condemned and controlled by societies everywhere in the world to an extent men cannot understand, cannot even imagine, not having felt it under our skin.

All the issues I have discussed—the establishment and collective enforcement of strict body standards, aversion to body fat, the construct of an ideal of beauty and the need to adhere to it, ageing—plus many others—dictates on what to and not to wear; the non-negotiable need to hide any natural imperfection or sign of tiredness behind makeup; the ruthless, imposed correlation between the look and manifestation of desires and sexuality—these and countless other cruel social rules weigh heavy on the shoulders of women who only want to be themselves. Men hardly scratch the surface of the pain and pressure.

It isn't hard to tell why: we have spent centuries treating women's bodies as objects under collective influence and control. As blank canvases for the manifestation of our aesthetic preferences and sexual desires, and instruments for the enforcement of our moral beliefs. And generation after generation, we have all been imposing boundaries of adequacy and an array of inferences and associations to every physical characteristic or individual choice. To look like a lady, to look like a whore. The countless labels that ultimately imply that we have the power to determine what a woman is. We do not.

From a position of privilege, it is hard to assess how much it hurts, and what is the way out of it. **Freedom today is harder for women. Perhaps it has always been.** But I am hopeful. And it's not without hard work, but it does seem like the world is changing. I think freedom is a two-way road; as we claim it for ourselves, we give it to everyone else. As we establish and concede the basic right to be as we are, we accept ourselves and we accept others. We feel accepted. So the more men and women discover that it is possible to be you, to be anything, the more we will look out, especially towards women, and fill our eyes with admiration. Amazed at the uniqueness of their individuality and forget that there was ever a standardized way to be. Hopefully.

. . .

There is a Buddhist teaching called the two truths: conventional truth and ultimate reality. In a nutshell, it distinguishes between everything that relates to our human experience, the *phenomenal world*—conventional truths—and a higher, absolute existence, the ultimate reality. How we experience and categorize the world, the names and meaning we give to everything, are conventional truths. They are conventional because they exist based on our mutual understanding of things and are only upheld *because* of that collective agreement: back to the chair, we look at it and agree that it is a chair, and that it is meant to be sat on.

Me, my family, my social circle and anyone I might meet understand and agree that I am Fabio, a man of a determined age counted in years, with a set of characteristics that identify me and that indicate certain things about myself as a human being. If our collective understanding of what being a man means fell apart and I was not considered one for whatever reason, I would no longer exist in that same form: Fabio, the man.

When Duchamp presented his urinal as a work of art, *Fountain,* in 1917, and intellectuals started to understand and agree that it was indeed artwork, that urinal ceased to exist as a urinal. A century later, even if you don't agree that a urinal should be considered art, the very question it puts before you makes it art itself. Even if you were to pee in it. And there is an object which transformed entirely, because its existence is a convention. The entire world, as we perceive it, is conventional.

It isn't hard to extrapolate. We look at someone who we deem fat, and as a society we collectively use the term "fat" to describe their physical condition. Then we apply all of our collective understanding of what fat means when assessing that individual. Or we all agree that looking young is a good thing, and that becomes a conventional truth. But, as the name says, these are conventions: none of them are, ultimately, reality!

Studying that concept, I started questioning the unmet goals and expectations that were leading to my continuous dissatisfaction with my career, my appearance, my relationships. I started trying to reprocess any frustration that came to my mind based on that idea: is this upsetting me because it has an objective, negative impact in my life, or because it goes against a "conventional truth?"

I don't believe these things happen as a coincidence, but at that same time I started reading a book called *Taste: The Secret Meaning of Things,* in which Stephen Bayley, the founder of London's Design Museum, explores the transforming meaning of tasteful through art and design history, much like Umberto Ecco did with beauty and ugliness. It goes without saying that what is considered good taste changes drastically through time. But I did learn that the word *taste* used to mean simply "discrimination," and was then transformed by cultural elites to arbitrarily describe their aesthetic choices and claim their superiority.

And Bayley explains further: "While I stop short of believing that all human affairs are no more than a jungle of ethical and cultural relativity, the suggestion that the infinite variety and vast sweep of the mind should be limited by some polite mechanism of 'good form' is absurd."

I had a huge epiphany reading his words. The lack of universal standards of aesthetic choice was being presented by an expert, someone who has dedicated his life to certifying the good from the bad. And he did a perfect job articulating the mindset I was exercising, triggered by my Buddhist practice: **all human affairs are no more than a jungle of ethical and cultural relativity.** It's hard to feel bad about yourself when all standards are put in that perspective.

If we are able to understand the conventional nature of the standards and norms we measure ourselves against, all the way down to the meaning of adjectives—beautiful, sexy, attractive—we come to the realization that we are not tied to them. That they are not part of our human constitution, that we can change them and see the world in any, any possible way. Our own way! We discover our power to certify the good from the bad ourselves, for ourselves.

We are living in times of dramatic changes in social dynamics, and the prospects look optimistic. I see people proud of the shapes of their bodies, no matter what they look like, and others who feel empowered to change it, for the sake of their own individual benefit. There is certainly an increasing diversity of shapes, colors and forms in the media, even though there is still a long way to go. Women are claiming their right to control their bodies, to wear what they want, to say no, to be satisfied sexually and to choose whether they shave. Overall, I think people do feel more beautiful, free. I see them bringing to our collective consciousness the fascism of standards and refusing to comply, simply by listening to themselves. Though not without insecurities.

I am far from making peace with my physical appearance. Some days I feel gorgeous, some days I feel like shit. More often I just feel, well, normal. Maybe that is, indeed, a biological human condition, and not a social artifact: we look at ourselves differently. Under a different light, or with different eyes. We look different, objectively. And should take the time to evolve, to welcome, to accept. As hard as the task continues to be, I keep on trying to put away the conventions, to empower myself, to be myself, happily. To turn off the noise and listen in. To smile at myself when I look in the mirror.

LOVE

One day I noticed that I did not seem capable of establishing a stable, long-term affectionate relationship. All my experiences were carefully built around my fears about sharing and my difficulties engaging with people—either long-distance, or with very loose and unclear boundaries, or just uncommitted. Bodies together, mind running solo.

At the rise of my 20s, as most of my friends had one or many boyfriends and girlfriends, I used to praise my choice of singledom, of rebellion against the romanticized, Hollywoodian love. I despised the notion of finding another half: I am a whole, I used to say, proudly! I observed people getting in and out of relationships that they only seemed to endure for the sake of not being alone—where I felt the most comfortable. It was hard to see the point. Like anyone, I also experienced a few heartbreaks, and further strengthened my disdain for the idea of a soulmate.

But time calms anyone down. We all experiment with positive—and not so positive—relationships, and we all crave companionship, at least. The nature of friendships changes, and eventually even the closest friends move on to walk their own paths. We move forward and around independently. I remember a feeling of always-there, of being together, of being with people—my people—for everything. But my people are, firstly, their own. No two paths are the same forever. We share them for periods, but will then age to inevitably become lonelier.

I started feeling the weight of loneliness while still guarding my inviolable space and my sense of independence. Consistently, though unconsciously, I avoided all relationships that seemed feasible. I felt increasingly attracted to anyone who showed lack of interest, and I turned off the more someone seemed to show they cared.

While actively looking to meet guys and connect, I shut down the ones who seemed to be hanging around for too long. Through different attempts, I discovered my complete inability to position myself emotionally in a relationship, speak about my feelings or communicate with a partner. I later understood that I had never learned to express how I feel. I avoided any conversation about being together, about the future or anything that bothered or concerned me within the context of a relationship. At the same time, I would pick small fights about things I didn't care about, a desperate attempt to show that I had feelings at all. Other couples seemed to argue, so I thought it was important. That being particular, or jealous, showed that I was present, that I cared. I didn't. As these psychological patterns surfaced to consciousness, I felt incapable of loving.

Meanwhile, people around me were meeting their soulmates, or their soulmates for the year (some souls mate for even less time). We loners start observing others' happiness together. We go to people's weddings, and cry. We go through Sunday evenings alone. We are the ones people call to drink and dance their sadness away when they break up—but their breakups don't last. We start contemplating a lonely old age, terrified.

My favorite of Clarice's characters, Lori, prays to God as she searches for herself and her place in the world: "May I let go of the modesty of hoping that, at the time of my death, there is a loved human hand to hold on to mine. Amen."

Watching and engaging with the world, we loners start to believe that there is something missing. That the choice of singledom can be a burden and that perhaps humans are indeed just halves, or at least very lonely wholes. In my case it felt worse, as I didn't it was possible for me to *ever* change that. Unable to open up, to connect, to share and to find myself truly involved. What do you do when you become increasingly certain there is something you need and increasingly certain you're not capable of having it?

I found myself a therapist. I came to him with a very straight-forward, well-articulated issue: I had found a gap that I needed to close. I seemed to want a relationship, yet was unable to establish it. So, we could either work to accept my instincts and understand that it wasn't for me, or fix the psychological triggers that got in the way of successful partnering. Whichever he'd think was easier. I felt sharp and mature, coming to therapy with such clarity over my struggles, different strategies to choose from. It would be quick and painless, and I would be a happy man—whether with someone, or alone.

His response, of course, was very different. No, I didn't understand my struggles or my way out of them. We started on a much different journey than I expected, longer and more nuanced. He didn't think I was inherently incapable of being in a relationship, nor that I had to suppress those wishes. He didn't think the problem was my challenges in connecting with people, though we did acknowledge and worked through many of those. The problem was in my—or everyone's—understanding of what being in a relationship means. It was both chasing and avoiding a notion of *being together* massified by everyone I watched out there.

He articulated: A meets B, they have things in common, they like spending time together and grow closer. That becomes, at some level, *a* relationship. But both already bring a very well-defined understanding of a dynamic, rules, habits and a "natural" evolution course for being together—all the components of *being in a relationship* that they established long before meeting each other. That they learned observing their parents, their friends, the movies. The collective understanding of relationships. So, A and B will move forward following an arrangement that completely ignores what they want to build with each other. It is quite likely that they don't even know what their individual preferences are when it comes to shared living.

As we discovered, what turned me off, even before I started getting involved with a specific individual, was the model, the format of most relationships I observed. That collective notion of what being together has to be. I disliked an idea of a present and future together that I built based on my observations of other people around me and through the media. One that is oblivious to who I am and what I want for myself. I took that for the norm, *the* definition of a relationship. And as much as I tried, deep inside, I didn't like it. I still don't.

But there was more: I also admired and envied couples' happiness without considering that I could only ever access a side of their lives together. The side they turn out to the world. Their challenges and struggles, their morning breath, their intimate uncertainties about being with each other, the pacts that they make, and that are only theirs—no one ever accesses, and yet no relationship comes without. A relationship between A and B only exists between A and B, no one else can possibly know how it functions, and thus cannot really envy it. It didn't take much reflection to corroborate this idea, thinking about the couples I am closer to. My parents, my brother and his girlfriend, close friends. Happy at some level, but not without struggles. Enjoying the best, but in constant exposure to the worst of each other. Winning some, losing some. Listening to the other snoring, sleeping in separate beds. Far from a life of pure bliss. Working hard to make it work.

Every movie, every song, every story we hear describes this exchange of souls, this once-in-a-lifetime finding, a breathtaking presence that will leave you without the slightest doubt: you found them. Reality is a lot more uncertain for most of us.

We deal with our own insecurities when we engage with someone sexually and affectionately, we may not be sure, we change our minds. And, too often, we realize that the everlasting passion extensively described by the poets wasn't a lasting state of completeness, but a quick flame that burns and goes. And then leaves us with something far from perfect, and questions and questions and questions.

. . .

The models, standards, values, and scripts that govern how we lead our affectionate and sexual lives seem to be more internalized than any other. Every society, past and present, has precise norms and expectations as to when and how people should connect—here, again, rules are stricter for women. We think and act like animals following a ritual to mate on the Discovery Channel: at what age should you have your first sexual experience, how frequently you should repeat (more for men, less for women). How many serious relationships you should have, and how long they should last. All while the clock ticks non-stop towards the deadline by when you should find *the one*—you will become absolutely undesirable past that (again, women perish earlier). Our entire life, predetermined.

We are all under enormous pressure to follow that pre-established timeline on the unrolling of our love lives. Needless to say, that timeline, applied to all, does not take into account our idiosyncrasies. Our preferences, our priorities, our fears, ourselves. If we want to focus on something else. If we simply don't like people. It just determines what our hearts should want, and when, and that it has to be able to find it, ignoring that hearts can't be pre-configured. It also ignores the uniqueness of our paths; the opportunities life will present us with—or the ones it will deny us. No observance or respect for the self: just a one-must-fit-all sequence of ticked boxes: single—committed—engaged—married...

The expectations start early, within our families. Long before they experience their animal instinct of procreating, women learn of their designated role in this world, to become mothers. Fulfilling that duty has a timing. And then the right times to kiss, to start dating, to be in and out of relationships, get engaged and married are all set. The chronology of our entire lives constantly reinforced by questions from relatives, the love lives of our friends, the media.

As in other spheres of our lives, these external forces, expectations, become our own individual objectives. They are at the core of a complex psychological system of die-hard goals (having children, finding someone before "getting too old"), the established method and timeline to deliver on them (adequate behavior, social norms, age), and pressure, frustration, anxiety.

We don't stop to wonder if those goals are aligned with our own desires, what we think will make us happy. The system prevents us from thinking about how we want to live our lives.

A few single girlfriends of mine, past their 30s, don't seem to be on track to follow the established path. They're rebels. Beautiful, independent, little to no experience with long-term relationships. The reasons vary: from the lack of interesting-enough opportunities, to personality, to not wanting to settle for less. But they don't live without struggles. They certainly fear never finding someone and feel like time is running through their fingers.

They will probably say their singledom is more due to lack of luck than to their own subconscious choices. And while they embrace their life of freedom, wear their independence with pride, I think they secretly hope that the world would turn and they'd fall back on the traditional path. They live with courage, but many insecurities. They hear jokes, question their own traits and behavior, worry about the future. They are unaware that how they live is actually connection with their inner nature. The uniqueness of a person's journey. Absolutely burdened by the pressures of a world that claims there is only one way to live.

Another friend, gay, mid-30s, heard from a 20-something boy on a dating app that it was sad that he was still looking for someone online at his age. He was devastated. He already felt he was running past his time. He wanted to find the one, but the one wouldn't want him if he was too old. In a way, he believed that online dating, at his age, was indeed kind of sad. But where is the threshold? Are the thousands, millions of over-30, over-40-year-old single men, women, gay, straight, bi—out there wondering if there is something wrong? And those who are, did they ever really want to be in a relationship? Or did the subconscious power of their essence guide their choices, their path to this day?

An article in the *New York Magazine* described the concept of "super singles." It had been coined by a character on a TV show, *Better Things*. It means someone who is single, but who built an "ecosystem" of people around them that fulfills all their needs for human connection, while remaining single. Someone who has learned to be good at being alone. "In the absence of another person, they have figured out how to be thriving, happy, unbothered, horny, fulfilled, and they don't want that disrupted." I smiled at the idea.

The key here is that "ecosystem." Some needs are indeed human, not social: companionship, support, sex, laughter, advice. But they don't need to be fulfilled by the same person. The one. They shouldn't; that would not only build a condition of super-dependence, it is also terribly burdensome on that individual. We don't all have super-single personalities. Many, probably most of us, do need the comfort of someone else by our side. But I think everyone could benefit enormously from building that ecosystem. And from doing some self-listening!

I recognize that women's genuine wish to have children poses an objective barrier on their bodies and their minds. Some of their concerns are, indeed, internal, and not internalized. But how much of that barrier has already been pushed by medicine? When we break with shared life standards, even the most objective, biological generalizations transform, and allow us to live more like ourselves. Today, women can become mothers without ever having a partner. They can get pregnant after they're 40. Or 50. They can raise their children without a father—sometimes better than with one. The pressures, the anxiety they still feel, are less because of the limitations of their reproductive system, and more, again, because of the pressure of artificial standards.

And it's not only women. It seems like people in general are becoming aware of the many possibilities of living together or alone, less constrained by the predetermined script. A couple of friends in their 30s were truly in love with each other, had similar interests and a happy life together. They shocked us when they told us they were breaking up. There were no incidents, no fights, love hadn't faded. They still liked each other but decided they shouldn't be together. They looked at the path they were on, still young and in love, and knew how it would unfold.

In that relationship for a few years, they already lived together and would soon start thinking about getting married, as per the script. They really did like each other, their life had been all mapped out. Except that they didn't want that. They came to understand they had not experienced enough. They had not lived enough. There was more to be seen, the inevitable commitment didn't seem to adjust to their thirst of living, of seeing the world. They got along so well that there was no way around it: together, they would get in the way of each other's human experience. And they parted ways. With their hearts broken, but their souls in peace. Free.

I was so touched by their story. So brave. So close to what I believe in: listening to yourself. Choosing for yourself. Not very long ago we couldn't—the official script and tradition were actually enforced. Not long ago there was a way we had to live. That is now becoming the way we *think* we have to live by. But the world has been making space for our individualities. As hard as it is to hear them through everything we are taught to believe in, they are always there.

. . .

Finally getting into a relationship doesn't mean being set free from the pressure of external expectations. The rules that govern most relationships are never built by the couples themselves, after carefully looking at their personal preferences and motivations for being together. Most couples outsource the principles guiding their lives together, establishing and enforcing dynamics that are largely oblivious to how they want to live with their partners. They simply follow the social norms that dictate how to love and live with someone.

When people do get together, whether for love, pressure or convenience, they follow a guidebook copied from their families, social circle, and the entire world out there. It outlines what being in a relationship means. What are the required behaviors, habits, and even feelings; the right way to love each other. We start taking in these external influences early, by watching our parents. Through reading, therapy and reflection, I was amazed by how much of the relationships we establish as adults mirrors what we grow up observing in our parents. Our conception of commitment and respect, our obligations and expectations, our behavior patterns. They are our first, our most important reference point for engagement with other human beings, and that's not necessarily a bad thing.

While our evolution does depend on incorporating structures, systems, and knowledge from previous generations, we should be *building upon them*. What is curious, or dangerous, is how we often grow up to repeat our parents' model of relationship, and all of their psychological triggers and responses entirely. Their misconceptions about being together, their mistakes, their unfounded rules. From within our homes we grow up watching our parents' struggles. Many of us watch the end of their relationships, their pitfalls as a couple, and yet, unconsciously, we believe that that is exactly how two people should live together.

My parents got married young and went on to live the same life. Partners at home, in business, in everything. They never, ever went out or did anything on their own, a weekend away, never made an individual decision. For over 30 years they have been sharing everything, sharing the same life. Growing up, my brother and I saw them as a unity, our parents, the two-pronged, but singular head of our family. And that seems to work well for them. But it's an idea that terrifies me—the suffocating perspective of giving myself up, letting go of the life I built solo. My space, my bed, my daily choices, my well-kept, subconscious freedom to pack my bags and leave at the tick of the slightest impetus. Hence my resistance.

But do all relationships mean absolute, unrestricted sharing? Are they all about concessions? Or is there *a* relationship that doesn't go against my nature of the all-sacred self? Obviously, relationships, on average, became more respective of individuals' spaces since my parents got married. Obviously, people are increasingly independent, while still part of happy couples. And obviously, those trends across time mean nothing, and the relationships I choose to build can be entirely about independence, all about exchanging, and not sharing. The relationships I choose to build don't have to be anything but *possible*, for me.

Couples I observe establish parameters for everything, from how often and what they talk about, to what they do together and what they do apart. Their sex lives and the pace of its decline, everything about their lives together, is based on what they think is appropriate from their social references. Adjusting and getting used to things that make them unhappy or unsatisfied, but paranoid with aspects of their relationships that seem to differ from those around them.

Assuming that their path together has already been laid out, that there is a right way to couple and that partner expectations are universal and obvious, many couples don't talk. They rarely communicate, they don't negotiate. Hardly ever discuss or present their individual personalities, wishes, desires and reasons for being with each other. They live governed by unspoken rules, swallowing dissatisfactions until they fight! It's beyond my individual experience, but I am genuinely surprised observing that many of the couples I know only ever state what they want and expect from each other when they can no longer take it, are under stress and in a conflict. For almost the entirety of their lives together, they are just relying on a model that is out there. No attempt to experiment, to explore. They begin and end their relationships following a script, without ever knowing what they came for.

Every couple out there is wondering if they have enough sex, concerned that they don't do it enough or ever, and no one is discussing the problem or a solution because it would tear down the myth that we all live happily just by following the norms. Individuals in couples would like more space for themselves, but they fear what that would do to the collective sense of being together. What wanting to be alone would state about their willingness to be with each other. They are arguing about how their neighbors make it home in time for dinner, but never conveying that they would like to feel more adventurous, more supported emotionally. Or more encouraged in their careers, more attuned with each other's desires, more loved as time passes by. There has to be a different way. Many different ways: for every couple, a different way of being together.

. . .

My friend Zizi and I were discussing open relationships, which may still seem like something from another world to straight couples, but have long been happily embraced by gays, thank you very much. People make all types of agreements in their attempt to set themselves free from the unjustifiable burden of living what they hope to be the rest of their days deprived from the chance of ever playing with a different set of genitals. It's healthy. They're happy.

While articulating that point I said, "So when two people get together and start an open relationship..." Zizi interrupted immediately: an open relationship isn't something you can start from scratch. It's something things evolve to, the outcome of exhausting your possibilities one-to-one. It is what couples try after being together for too long exclusively. If you're proposing to be open from the get-go, do you even want to be together? Do you love each other at all? I agreed.

Later, thinking of his interjection, it occurred to me, how far-reaching, how ingrained in our thinking are our norms and standards when it comes to love. Zizi and I are open-minded people, we believe in freedom. Here we were openly discussing an idea that is, in itself, somewhat revolutionary. Unusual at least. And here we are curbing it with a set of rules on its own terms. Open-minded, but still trying to standardize. The meaning of everything has already been determined, one way or the other.

Even for those who eventually give in to the need to change, to accept, to transform.

The human heart was made to love one individual at a time, period. Until not very long ago, the human heart was made to love one individual *ever,* period. That is our most ubiquitous, immutable truth. The suggestion that a person can genuinely love two or more people at the same time is absurd. Even worse, the possibility of living more than one love simultaneously is immoral, sinful, dirty, slutty, inconceivable. No convention or rule is so deeply rooted in our mindset as the limits of the human capability to love.

Monogamy in our Western world is taken for granted. So much so that we never, ever think about it or question its prevalence. We don't question the basis for love and sex that can only be between two people, ever. As that has been established as fundamental law, we all struggle to reconcile our own evolving desires, and calibrate our expectations towards others, without much flexibility to love and let love. We don't consider that monogamy might, itself, be nothing more than a social construct—and one that doesn't seem to be in line with our human instincts. Because of that construct, we feel guilt, we suffer, we hurt others—and judge.

David P. Barash, a zoologist and psychologist, and Judith Eve Lipton, a psychiatrist, investigated the idea and prevalence of monogamy in animals and human beings. Their research on evolutionary biology was published in *The Myth of Monogamy: Fidelity and Infidelity in Animals and Humans*, and they are categorical to conclude that "there is simply no question whether desire for multiple partners is 'natural,'" as well as "no question of monogamy being 'natural.' It isn't." The scientists used DNA mapping technology to track mating across species with fascinating findings. The best of them: that while bonobos, *Homo sapiens'* closest genetic relatives, live in a "nonstop sexual free-for-all," there is a species of fish-parasite flatworm that partners up before their biological sexual awakening and remain together, until death.

So there is no biological basis for monogamy in human beings, and anthropological, social, and historical factors led us to believe that one-to-one is the only way. That may sound groundbreaking for some. Even more inspiring than their research, I found, is their book's epigraph, a quote from English philosopher Francis Bacon: "The world is not to be narrowed till it will go into the understanding (...), the understanding to be expanded and opened till it can take in the image of the world, as it is in fact."

A dear friend of mine loved two men. She never told me, but I knew she did. Wholeheartedly. She had been in a loving, fulfilling relationship for years, when she met this other guy. And he loved her back. Because of her discretion, I was left to imagine how far their involvement went, physically and emotionally, but I watched a friend become scared, almost devastated by the audacity, the rebellion of her heart. Interestingly, I don't think her suffering came from traditional heartbreak, from recognizing that the fulfilment of her desires was not socially feasible. It wasn't about having to choose, letting go of genuine love. Her upset was to observe her own heart and mind break against the unquestionable limitations we've placed on human love. Perhaps it would have been easier if she had, more naturally, met someone and stopped loving the previous, changed her heart. Channeled her feelings towards the new. Broken up, ran away, let go. But feeling for both at the same time? Genuinely having that extra love to give? That cannot be.

    Today we are prepared to accept infidelity. We may overcome being deceived, lied to, we will rise from being humiliated. We may be able to forgive almost anything—the most disrespectful, inconsiderate behavior. Looking around, we hear and witness the most disgusting stories of heartbreak with a disturbing sense of normalcy. But we cannot possibly conceive, we can't accept that someone truly loves more than one person.

    How can we incorporate an idea to the extent of allowing it to challenge our most natural animal behavior? That we reject, deny and fight against our human instincts? How can it seem so wild, when it's nothing but our nature? How powerful are our social constructs, how distant are they from our essence, how unhappy can they make us?

I may be optimistic, but I like to think that this is hardly provocative, that it's almost obvious, a sort of instinct of survival: to make an effort to set aside the norms passed from generation to generation, the flawed morals from religion and the state. The fear of the close watch of our neighbors to find, perhaps buried and dusty, who we are and what we like.

This is not to dismiss, by any means, the bond between two people who chose to be partners for life, or for as long as they feel like, or to discourage the pursuit of a one-to-one affectionate and sexual, intimate relationship. Monogamy is not bad, or impossible. It is not an attempt to encourage polyamorous lifestyles, or to suggest that they are, in any way, better or more suitable for anyone. This is a statement on the relativity, the deep unimportance of our most strongly-held beliefs that, torn down, make way for multiple possibilities for living—or for truly appreciating the status quo.

The possibilities of love beyond monogamy are, perhaps, the most controversial idea I can introduce. The wildest. Without the need to encourage them: just by acknowledging their existence. And yet I think it is the most natural. And, because it shocks, it might be the one that matters the most.

Understanding the relativity of *all* the constructs that govern our living with no mercy, no space, no respect for our idiosyncrasies, is the only path I can see towards freedom. Towards a life of better understanding, of ourselves and others. Of more love, for ourselves and others. While we want and work for love to be a direct, one-way-only transfer of feeling and intimacy, it can be many and multi-directional, it can be fluid, it can be whatever we want.

Social constructs and artificial standards do have the power to put us in true psychological prisons. While they can restrain plans, thoughts and desires, some mental effort and the possibilities of our reality might, openheartedly, unchain us from the myth of one-love-only. They might open the doors to a lifetime of experimentation. Perhaps throughout time—or maybe at the same time, because we can. That idea of limitless love is the only definition of love truly unconditional: not only unlimited by another individual's behavior and characteristics, but entirely unattached from any individual at all. Love, purely. In itself, in us.

. . .

Zizi and I were catastrophizing, though not entirely unsubstantiated, about the complexity of our love lives. Liking and being liked at discrepant levels. Wanting different things from different people. Longing something and not being sure of what that is. Moments of joy leading to abrupt emotional chaos. Feeling overwhelmed, then feeling incomplete.

We laughed at searching for or obsessing over people who clearly didn't have the potential to make us happy in any way. For months. Looking for sex in people who wanted love, and for love in people who only wanted sex. Changing our hearts, hypothesizing about the impossible, leaving people on hold, "ghosting" and "being ghosted". And we noticed an underlying thread that was common to all the bliss and the drama: an absolute lack of clarity. Not really, ever, knowing what we were looking for.

Without establishing an intent, just throwing ourselves at experiences, at people, with effort and energy. Sometimes even hurting others without really knowing where we are taking our own hearts. Claiming to want something, without knowing if it's something we would actually like to live with. Disregarding consequences. And then behaving in a completely different way. Our love lives seemed more like a lost kite blowing loosely in the wind than a boat under the control of a guiding captain, heading to a destination—*any* destination. And we resented that.

It certainly seemed possible to feel more fulfilled if we were moving towards a goal. If we could channel desires, behavior, actions. It would be so productive to focus, to make sure that every thought, every word is a driving force leading us somewhere. It is worth the exercise: examining our engagement with other people, always asking, "What is this for?" At the very least, making sure our relationships, until-death-do-us-part or for one-night-only, are doing us some good. We can consciously do that.

After all, self-understanding is the key to freedom. Know thyself. But we cannot always. At the limit of our ability to establish where we are going is the undeniable fact that living is a process of experimentation. Of trial and error. Of pushing boundaries. Of making mistakes. We are complex creatures! We can't get to our essence, we can't expect to accomplish our human existence, on the first try. It has to hurt!

So I feel like we have to, first of all, respect other people, non-negotiably. Then, increasingly, become aware of what seems to make us happy, of where our behavior is taking us, of where we might see ourselves in the future. But ultimately, letting go. Acknowledging that we won't always know why or what for. Throwing ourselves into the arms of the human experience, with all of its confusion, its soft spot for heartbreak, its nonlinear paths. Trying fearlessly, shamelessly.

I realize that my dissatisfactions, frustration and unhappiness aren't coming from my own failed experiments with love and sex. They are coming from a blind belief that I am not moving forward on the way that has been established. The path others seem to walk. They are not to do with accomplishment, but with expectations. That dissatisfaction is not to do with failed or unfocused experimentation with love. It is rather a non-experiment: outsourcing our understanding of a happy life, instead of going and figuring it out ourselves.

Honestly, our idea of love is so limited—and so limiting! How much more, how much better are we able to give and take, free from what has been taught? How much bigger and more complex are our hearts? How creative can we be when we establish who, when, and how we love? And if we understand the breadth of those possibilities, the ability to live according to our own perspective, how much happier will we be? Loving with honesty, either our other half exclusively, or half the world.

LIFE ONLINE

I was living in Munich and a friend took me for a day-long hike through the Bavarian Alps, where from the top we had beautiful views of Germany on one side and Austria on the other. The green hills went up and down for as far as the eyes could see, until the clouds met them on the horizon, and turquoise water held between them formed countless, bright little lakes surrounded with pine trees.

It was grand and beautiful, one of these times when the Earth makes you feel small before the vastness of nature but blessed for being able to witness it. We were still in awe of the entire experience when we finished the trail, but the ecstasy didn't last long for me. When we stopped at a restaurant for water, I took out my phone to go through the dozens of stunning pictures we had taken, the registry of the experience, only to find out that none of them had been saved. Because of some bug, the camera's software had captured the images, but not stored them. I could see their thumbnails, but they simply didn't exist as full-size files.

That very concept was hard for me to understand, being, myself, far from the world's most tech-savvy. I could see the pictures in some form, they must have been somewhere! But the more research I did, the more I went through long hardware forums, the more obvious it became, there were no pictures. Desperate, I called a techie friend, who confirmed the prognosis within minutes of his own, better informed research.

I spent all evening devastated, when I had a sudden moment of clarity. I looked at myself at the end of an incredible day spent doing one of the things I enjoy the most. I had been close to nature on a beautiful summer morning, under the sun, watching an impressive landscape I had never seen similar. And I was feeling upset. Why was that? I've never been particular about gathering and keeping memories, and yet it felt like, without the pictures, the experience didn't exist at all. And I realized that my frustration with that day was simply not being able to publicize it.

It was an awakening. An avid social media user, I thought of the many occasions when I went on trips and couldn't rest until I had the perfect shot. How much time I had wasted testing filters on pictures. How much thinking I would put into the frequency, the timing, the content I should post on social media. How I counted anxiously how many people liked the things I shared, and how I got upset when they got less attention than I was previously used to. How much energy I was dedicating to building that image of *a* self and how, at the end of the day, it all meant nothing. Absolutely nothing. That constant thirst for attention, the need to present a well thought-through positioning out to the world: nothing.

I deleted my accounts on social media, which at the time consumed so much of my time and my energy. And I didn't miss them for a second. In fact, I felt liberated.

. . .

In 1959 Canadian sociologist Ervin Goffman introduced, in a book called *The Presentation of Self in Everyday Life*, his now famous "dramaturgical perspective on social life." It is a metaphor comparing all human interactions to a theater play. In his analysis, we are all social actors, and life is made up of a backstage, hidden from the eyes of others, and a stage, where we perform the different roles that make up our identities. Through different sets (our homes, offices, bars, restaurants) we take on different parts (husband, father, professional). We engage with other performers and we are observed by an audience, as we build and adapt ourselves as individuals according to the different settings life gives us.

In our everyday lives, we social actors will manage every aspect of how we present ourselves to create a specific impression on our audience. We chose our clothes, words, mannerisms, posture and behaviors to portray ourselves as the characters we incorporate. Within a given *part*—husband, or business executive, or gay man—we will refer back to social norms and values to perform our *role*: the script, our words, and actions, in a careful attempt to shape how we are perceived. We ultimately want to influence how others behave towards us.

The goal of this meticulous performance is to be accepted, to have the audience believe in the individual we want to be, to be seen as we want to be seen. As human beings, we want to be respected. To be admired. To be loved. The unconscious goal of every detail in how we present ourselves and interact with others: to determine how they will perceive us and behave towards us.

When I invested, studied and worked to build a respectable career, got up from my chair and unconsciously forced a deeper tone to speak to a client; the many hours I spent at the gym and the food I avoided with my mouth watering, or ate with distaste; controlled and enhanced mannerisms, height-increasing insoles, my laughter. All mechanisms to influence how, in a specific context, the world looks at me and treats me back.

The challenge for us actors is to be consistent in our roles, to maintain the foundations of our characters through every situation, effectively striving to become those selves at all times. Goffman highlights, for instance, the risk of "breaking character," or being accidently observed in one of our backstage moments, when we are not wearing the traits we would like to put out to the world. Perhaps we are not quite as strong as we are seen to be? Not as skinny as we make our figures show? Not as wealthy as we like to make believe? It isn't easy to convince an observing audience that you are, indeed, that self you portray throughout an entire life. Or it wasn't in 1959.

Of course, at that time, there was no social media. Instagram, Facebook, Twitter, LinkedIn and others came to solve the great challenge of Goffman's dramaturgical social living, letting us deliberately determine how we are perceived, and influencing others' behavior. By setting social interactions free from the scrutiny of the audience's presence, they allowed us to choose when and how we are observed. To stage our performances more carefully, more deliberately, to pick the good side of our asymmetric face. To photoshop. After all, it matters little, if at all, if our characters hold any resemblance with reality. We pose. We filter. We edit. We spin. We convey beauty, wealth, intelligence, culture, happiness.

We became more aware of the performative essence of our social interactions, replacing the subconscious subtleness of our previous presentation efforts for deliberate, shameless posts aimed to project *a* self out to the world. As our social lives take place increasingly online and our control over the identity we convey increases, social actors today can become obsessed with their images. Caught between insecurity about our real selves and narcissism over our perfected characters, we build a careful online presence to satisfy our need for human connection.

Interestingly, while aware of everyone's power to shape their identity so meticulously, to hide the many pitfalls and imperfections of reality, we measure ourselves against those portraits of perfection presented online by others. Actors ourselves, we do understand that characters are constructed, that they are polished, framed, airbrushed to tell a crafted story. But we look at others' narratives as if they were real tales of success that we, ourselves, failed to achieve.

Goffman, already at that time, looked at the complexity of being both actors and audience. He noted that, as observers, we are willing to overlook the mistakes in others' compositions, so that we can believe in our own characters. Acknowledging their slips would be acknowledging that the play is not life itself. That our roles, too, are staged. For the sake of upholding the constructed reality we live in, our own peace of mind, and for us to believe in ourselves, as we would like to be, we believe in others.

However, we can't always wear the mask, not when we look in the mirror. We might be willing to overlook others' imperfections, but we can't run away from our own. The outcome? An unsatisfied world of people unavoidably aware of their own individual flaws, comparing themselves with a perceived perfection of the lives of everyone else.

. . .

With the use of social media we started to believe that everything needs to be publicized. I remember it starting innocently, with pictures of beautiful plates of food and resting feet before an ocean background. And it evolved to post-workout pictures.

Lengthy, obsessive political commentary. Countless hashtags. Growing follower bases and the ability to monetize them. A detailed coverage of day-to-day life. We all ended up developing an oversharing mindset, becoming part of an unhealthy exchange where we consume irrelevant, unrealistic, narcissistic content, while creating and sharing our own. We establish and engage in networks of aesthetic, cultural, and intellectual show-offs, purely to access a growing pool of individuals' staged perspectives, and to put out our own framed version of ourselves, in attempt to assert our self-worth within the captivating dynamic.

But that exchange, what I like to call the collective ego jerk off, is not the problem: it is a symptom. As it happens, when we live to fulfill a collective, outsourced idea of happiness, when we pursuit goals that we never came up with, but have been established by others, we do not feel entitled to account for their accomplishment ourselves. When we outsource the meaning of happiness, we also have to outsource its assurance. We need others to look at the life we've built and agree, collectively: that is what we all call happiness. For ourselves, we never defined what is enticing in the first place. For as long as we dedicate our lives to chasing after dreams, after objectives that were not established entirely by ourselves, after a lifestyle that is oblivious to our own instincts, we will need the world to evaluate how well we are doing. We won't be able to feel happy through our own individual confidence. Social media are only providing a platform for that constant, ongoing, ever-unfulfilling social assessment.

We are suddenly no longer able to determine whether we feel accomplished, we cannot account for our own satisfaction, we struggle to recognize our own value. We need others to watch how we live and, through their likes and comments, assure that we are doing well. It happens across countries, demographics and social classes. People of all kinds seem to think more and more that their joy only counts if it's made public.

It cuts across all spheres of life. We are seeking to validate everything that, due to its disconnection with our nature, does not seem to have the power to make us happy in itself. We publicize our professional lives using fancy vocabulary and overblowing achievements. LinkedIn and Twitter are filled with experts in nothing exercising the "top voice" they established often only by keeping talking. We must talk about our knowledge about everything and how cultured we are, the great books we read and plays we see, the breadth and depth of our thinking. For everything for which we lack confidence, we seek others' validation.

People publicize their happiness with their partners with constant, exaggerated, public declarations of love and unnecessary detail of their intimate life as a couple. They publicize their wealth, to the extent that it is appropriate (or not), through clothes, travel, and the right Instagram filters. Our taste, our eye for the beautiful, our aesthetic flair. All these categories of social values and standards unconsciously transformed into our individual goals and priorities. They all need others' eyes to become meaningful for ourselves. So we publicize success at work, money, love. And more than anything, by virtue of the media's format, we publicize our look.

Because of the pace of our times and our shrinking attention span, we are becoming more and more visual. As the interfaces of many social media platforms make clear, they're made to look at images. And social media became, to a large extent, windows for the exposure of our physical appearance. The airbrushing tools, the filters, the lighting, all facilitate the construction of better-looking, or rather more standard-conforming figures. We are now able to share how well we fit in with an unprecedented reach. Celebrities and so-called influencers found their place of prominence in this universe of vanity. Often more because of their luck and some sense of opportunity than the relevance of their work, they fuel the engine that makes all of us, known or unknown, admirers, seekers, exhibitors, and reinforcers of a notion of beauty. We must show our six-packs so the world can assure us that having one is important. So that it can reward our hard effort.

I find it kind of funny—if not boring—how even the aesthetics of the content people share are very similar: the framed backgrounds, the carefully rehearsed spontaneous shots and the many, many versions of selfies, whether through a mirror or on-your-face. **The selfie became, in a way, the ultimate token of social media and our desperate call for attention and validation: an image that says nothing, tells no story, but simply begs: look at me!**

Fremdschämen is a German word that describes a deep feeling of embarrassment on behalf of someone else. We have a version in Portuguese, *vergonha alheia*, something like alter-shame. If I go through people's social media these days, it is exactly what I feel. Perhaps that's how people would feel if they looked at mine. The presumption of others' interest, the tone of self-importance, the careful air of carelessness. Ridiculous is a word in English that describes a lot of what I see. Text that starts with "I'm humbled to…" and on and on about awards and achievements. Lessons learned through an incredible career journey. Pictures looking out at the horizon. Pictures in bed. Duck face. Look of the day. Check ins. Lack of shame.

These are the output of a world where people are increasingly conceited, insecure and unhappy—as paradoxical as that might sound. Conceited because of the constant interest, near-obsession, with our own achievements, how we are perceived, and with our public image. Insecure because that conceit doesn't come from a traditionally narcissistic, self-admiring mindset; it is just the product of the ongoing, collective ego jerk off. In fact, the posting and the need for likes and followers are a symptom of lack of genuine self-admiration. Of confidence. And unhappiness because, of course, the collective approval doesn't change the fact that the values behind what we exhibit are not idiosyncratic, they are not legitimate. They do nothing for the individual deep within, but to drive them to seek more and more compliance with the pre-established, right type of life.

. . .

Through content exchange, social media became platforms for the reinforcement and enforcement of all collective values and standards. They provide daily reminders that there is a right way we should be living and pre-established goals we should be achieving. On the one hand, they make us obsessed with the image we project, seeking constant validation through the content we put out. On the other, they are flooding our minds with those social standards and goals through the content we take in.

Interestingly, the reservoir of collective ideals social media platforms are providing is entirely artificial. Other people's entire lives, their professional success and adventurous lifestyle, the perfect portrait of their relationships and, again, how they look, are a carefully curated narrative, painting the picture of *a* life of achievement. The pictures, videos, texts and all other types of media are not a documented story of success and joy, but someone else's attempt to convey perfection and to be admired. At the very best, they might be honest snapshots of the prime moments of an otherwise normal individual's life—one just like ours.

What we access and go on to measure ourselves up against does not show other people's dissatisfaction at work and carefully negotiated job-title inflation. They don't show couples' uncertainties about each other and the many times when we, inevitably, hurt and feel hurt. They don't show financial struggles at the end of the month, guilt, cellulite. Most importantly, they don't show how unfulfilled people who dedicate their lives to crafting that online narrative feel inside. The material for comparison we are constantly exposed to and rely on is entirely unrealistic.

Belgian intellectual and academic Phillippe Dubois has the perfect analysis of photography's role in documenting the world and representing reality: it is "not like the world, it transforms the world." He sees a photograph not as a "trace-image-of-what-was-there," but a "fiction-image-of-a-world-possible." And there is no better way to describe the material, photographic or not, that we consume on social media. We look at it as if it were documentation of reality, as trace-images of others' lives. We perceive it as examples we should look up to and pursue and evidence that we are lagging behind and incomplete. But it is nothing but fiction. Staged, transformed images of a life that may be possible.

Pictures, text or videos on social media are like someone's resume. They show things that are (possibly) true in some form. They are (hopefully) somehow based on real aspects of individuals' lives. But they are presented in a way that will convey the character those people want to build. Framed to look better, edited and re-edited, exaggerated. They are an exercise in flexing the boundaries of real life to make an impression.

It is certainly not the case that all people are fake, or that most are obsessed with impressing the world. Not all posts on social media are desperate calls for appreciation. I rather think that what we see, and become part of, is a collective effort to fit in, to conform. To live up to the collective values of social circles, to seem engaging and, ultimately, worthy of connection. But we have to be careful, skeptical even, when we look at others' lives to make an assessment on our own.

This is where we find ourselves: looking not within, but to the world outside, to understand what it is that makes us happy within, and thus what we should pursue. Spending our days watching examples of individuals who seem to have actually achieved those goals. And reinforcing that misconceived idea of happiness. Feeling unachieved and disregarding both that we are comparing ourselves to fiction AND that neither we, nor the others, have established that those are the attributes that will make anyone happy. In fact, our social system of values and beliefs are so alienated from individuals that that so-called ideal life probably isn't truly ideal for any one person in the world.

Additionally, the examples we look up to are so sad! So uninteresting! The celebrity culture from the mass-media age evolved into the anxiety-filled "influencer" culture of our social-media age. While before an individual's fame was the outcome of their work in the arts, sports, fashion or whatever, influencers' fame comes purely from... influencing. Their lack of talent gives everyone the illusion that a "perfect" life crafted out of thin air is possible. The illusion that the values we see represented, whether beauty or money, are relevant, fulfilling, and easily achievable.

There is now a company that rents out private jets for a couple of hours so individuals can come in and take pictures for their social media profiles. The planes never take off! I didn't want to believe it, but people pay to have a chance to show others that they fly privately when they don't! And as if that wasn't enough, they bring different sets of clothes to change into, to make sure they can convey that it's recurrent, and not a one-time thing.

We can't get to the status of professional experts, specialists, speakers, motivators or consultants without having actually dived deep into the corporate experience. Our comments on politics are nothing but the view of a voter in the context we live in, not the perspective of political scientists or operators, people who truly understand society, the complexity of policy-making and the rules of power. And it is very unlikely that we will ever spend our lives between yachts and private jets, even though the current, very tacky lexicon of social media imagery is trying to turn them commonplace.

But even if that was all easy or possible, becoming business gurus, or intellectuals, or flying privately are not things that *matter*, or that help anyone feel accomplished as a human being. Whether some people get there or not, their positions have no absolute importance from a perspective of value assigned *within*. The achievements people share and the beauty of their travels matter only to them. Or at least we should hope they do.

What we interpret as others' lives from what we see online is strengthening money, success and beauty as our common measures of value, and making us feel like we are missing out. There is no happy ending to the collective ego jerk off, and the more those values and beliefs are cemented in our minds, the more natural, more absolute they feel. The further apart we grow from discovering the direction we would like to be traveling, by ourselves.

. . .

At the core of my belief is the idea that we must all, consciously, make the effort to understand what makes or has the potential to make us happy, idiosyncratically, and pursue it fearlessly. All values, expectations and parameters that might stand in our way are entirely relative and often irrelevant social constructs, rather than humankind fundamentals. So if someone was to test that argument to its own limit they could claim: I have become aware of my own wishes, and I am happier following every possible norm society establishes and reestablishes. Resigned, I would have to admire them, and recognize their ability to thrive, entirely against what I have come to understand as a path to human fulfillment. The upholding of any, absolutely *any*, path to happiness as a real possibility is relative to the subjectivity of the individual. I believe without restrictions that advice, reflections and life tips only matter, they can only be *good,* before the trial of a specific person. The principle of my entire understanding is that no direction is universal—certainly not my own.

However, there might be an exception, one thing that I have been thinking absolutely all humans could benefit from. This is somewhat like my take on "wear sunscreen": we need to put our phones down. Me, my family, all of my friends, every single person I observe over the course of my days should spend less time playing with their phones.

At the gym I used to see people using their phones on their breaks between exercises. Today, I see people typing obsessively *while* exercising. It's a little ridiculous, the ass in the air and the thumbs going wild. Let's not even mention tables at restaurants and bars. Men peeing at urinals, one hand in assistance, the other handling the phone. Not occasionally—all the time. I suspect women do it too, with both hands.

People are on their phones while working constantly—police officers on the street call my attention the most, and I see them everywhere. I honestly don't even understand what we spend so much time doing. I often catch myself by surprise having wasted time, sometimes hours, running late to something yet again, after having done nothing but use my phone. We seem numbed, hypnotized by their bright screens. The content on them is almost irrelevant, the phone is the end, no longer the means.

We check for messages and emails constantly, with online communications dictating the rhythm of our days. There is no longer a selection of applications for us to use when needed, but rather crowds of humans living to check and update mobile applications. The phone is the first thing we reach for in the morning and the last thing we put aside at night.

Using the phone is becoming the world's number one occupation, whatever we spend our times doing while we swipe and tap on touch screens. It is, without question, our primary source of services, information, knowledge and entertainment. It is also becoming our primary source of human connection. But there is more. It is not only a core, daily activity in itself, but the enabler of many others, the way through which people live—at shows, concerts, museums, galleries, weddings, people experience art and the world not through their eyes and pores, but through the lenses of their phones.

My belief that this piece of advice might be universal, and not relative, comes from an understanding that human life—for all humans—is a sensorial experience. We become aware of the world and of ourselves by observing, by being present. At times, when it seems so important to dedicate ourselves to thinking and understanding ourselves and others, we seem to be constantly plugged into a virtual existence, effectively seeking distraction from life.

While someone could indeed claim that their phone and their online habits make them happy, I'd be skeptical that they're not missing out on a better life offline.

. . .

Social media are, all things considered, a force of good. They allow people to connect and stay connected and bring us closer. They open opportunities and the windows of the world, and allow us to remain part of people's lives, regardless of time and distance. The problem is not in the platforms. The problem is how we chose to use them—or worse, not making any active choice at all.

For instance: why do we share things? Because we want to be in touch with and part of people's lives, to inspire, or because we need to validate our choices and achievements? And why do we observe? Do we feel inspired, are we driven to think and do things differently? Do we grow, or are we just reinforcing standards?

A friend of mine seemed to prove my reservations and theory all wrong. Intriguingly, she is on all social media platforms, uses them quite a lot, and seems to have established a perfectly healthy relationship with them. She genuinely seems to use them happily.

So I observed, talked to her, and thought again about my apocalyptic views of life online. I noticed that she understood and accepted, first and foremost, the key purpose of sharing moments of her life with people she loves and watching their moments back. She also realizes the potential to meet like-minded people, to make connections and to build a bridge between her online communities and real life. Finally, she acknowledges that social media can provide an infinite pool of inspiration, new ideas, concepts, legitimately interesting content on all things that interest her: travel, photography, nature.

None of what she sees, however, becomes a source of comparison with her own life. It only helps her dream. She doesn't ask herself questions. She doesn't obsess with what she is sharing. How could she, I wondered? What was the secret for understanding things so clearly, putting everything in their right place and not getting into the ego jerk off, the cycle of social standards?

And I realized that the secret wasn't in her relationship with social media: it was in her relationship with herself. Sofia happens to be one of the most self-assured, confident, positive people I know. She is fully aware of her goals and her sources of pleasure, of what and where she wants to be, and she enjoys living—though not without her personal struggles. She has always inspired me.

She told me innocently: "I don't understand people who keep their online profiles private... shouldn't they be channels for us to engage with people and to show the beauty in our everyday? To open up to the world?" Sofia feels no need for likes and followers, for assurance, for validation. There is no self-loathing before the artificial lives of others. Just an endless thirst for engaging with the world. Her method: just being fully aware of her (own) *self*.

When we live on autopilot, just following the protocols and the already-established paths, we neglect our ability to make choices and tune the world to our own functioning. We stop making things work for us and fall into the traps of collective assumptions. Everyone else seems to behave a certain way, so we simply go along. They use social media to show their achievements and acknowledge the achievements of others. An important part of their social lives takes place online. And we just follow suit. We don't question or wonder what our individual purpose for being there is, what we can make out of our lives online and how we can put them to work to make us happy. The world is to be molded.

Tools and technology exist to serve us in any way that suits us better—they shouldn't be systems for increasing massification. On the contrary, they should, and are, giving voice to the dissents, the revolutionaries, the rebels, all of us who feel, consciously or unconsciously, disturbed by that need to follow suit and fit in.

EPILOGUE

While I had managed to find some peace, I kept looking for every resource to better understand life and to find answers to my many questions, old and new. To better understand whether there is a path towards satisfaction and to connect with myself. To find my true freedom, one that would be once and for all. Buddhism, therapy, God, volunteer work, ayahuasca, mindfulness, friends, and constant, ongoing reflection on the human condition.

After all the years of incompleteness and my seamless inability to feel truly free, I started realizing that there wasn't anything that could fill my successive gaps and pitfalls. No way out of my frustrations. My concerns regarding work and career.

My physical appearance. My love life and engagement with other people and many, many others seemed to be a constant part of living. Every time I managed to step out of an issue, another source of emptiness would come up. It was then when it started to become clearer that the solution wasn't to satisfy every frustration, to fill every gap. The only possible escape would be to make some kind of peace with my dissatisfactions, to somehow reframe them so we could live alongside.

To understand my frustrations better, I had to understand myself better. Carl Rogers believed that all human beings live under a curious paradox: that it is only when we accept ourselves fully, openheartedly, as we are, that we are able to change. I started to dig deeper into my issues to try to find where they were coming from, while mapping out where I really wish I was in life. And that was when I first started taking notice of my intrinsic wishes and beliefs and realizing the disconnection between them and my lifelong pursuits.

While working to become aware of some of the things I did want, and the many things I didn't want, with the help of therapy, I went on a period of intense reflection on the dynamics of processing life. Observing a lot, feeling a lot, both hopeful and sad, confident and weak, I deliberately stopped and took the time to go through every little experience, through each of my days. And my mind seemed to always return to the ideas of **negligence**

towards my individuality, the irrelevance of the standards and parameters by which I was guiding my life and **infinite choices and human possibilities**. They were recurring, coming back to me while processing every struggle, in every aspect of living. Or every time I came in contact with the struggles of friends or people around me.

But at first, they were just thoughts. Attempts to understand my feelings better, to make peace with myself. I didn't have any revelation, I just noticed that listening to myself, acknowledging the relativity of my internalized goals and the existence of many other possible paths, while not exactly answering all of my questions, offered some relief. It seemed to provide me with that perspective to rethink my frustrations and emptiness. But I still didn't have a clear framework to process the many questions I have about living.

So I decided that, to understand that call for transformation in my mind, I had to articulate it. I needed to structure, logically, what those three ideas meant, and their potential as tools for peace of mind, satisfaction, and happiness. I started writing about them. I pulled together all the thoughts that seemed to point in the same direction, my own little stories, other people's experiences, theory, advice, everything. Testing happiness and dissatisfaction in the contexts of self-respect and social expectations. It was through these thought experiments, looking back at my trajectory, that I was able to connect those three ideas, and the underlying thread of finding freedom—my personal, primary quest as a human.

As those thoughts were taking shape, I realized that writing them down didn't only help me understand them, it helped me *accept* them. It helped me exercise happiness. It pushed me to effectively reframe living, to distance myself from the heat of emotions and context, to go through my human processes with more awareness and maturity. The way we understand and plan our lives is so rooted in our social experience, with every step seeming so obvious, that complying just happens unconsciously. Stepping out to think for yourself is a challenge like no other, no matter how well you understand a new paradigm, rationally. And that was how this book started.

Reading back on these thoughts, I resent that they come out as if I have everything figured out. Like all human emptiness seemed hacked through reconnecting essence and effort. Like I had learned how to do it myself. That couldn't be farther from the truth. All the ideas I present are concerns I struggle with daily. I was simply trying to convince myself. Not intellectually, but through experience. These notes are, in themselves, an exercise in listening to myself better, in practicing my conscious beliefs and putting aside the many, deep preconceptions I have on life and how it should be lived.

EPILOGUE

. . .

Many, large windows opened before me, and they showed the world I knew once in a very different way. They let unprecedented light in and looked out to my infinite possibilities and my own ability to transform. They looked out to a life crafted entirely by the burning desires of my own heart and to large crowds of different people and their own very different hearts and desires.

Through them I saw that if I was able to listen to myself, to understand my true nature, nothing, absolutely nothing could stand between me and my own truth, my realization. All obstacles, all shackles were social and psychological constructs, illusions that I could make disappear simply through thinking.

And I started to believe that freedom is indeed a real possibility, not way ahead in the future, but today. That if my limitations are relative and not concrete, if all standards are social and not biological, it should take pure reframing inside to tear them down—even though that is a very hard task in itself. Still, life could be good without any fights against conventions, no one else to convince. No battles or revolution, no changing of circumstances. Only reframing within.

Under that new light, I observed both my concerns and the choices before me more consciously, and the brightness lets me contemplate the breadth of the endless directions that lie ahead if I allow myself to think with true freedom. I started listing down all the possible paths I could see, roads in and out of self-realization, or of chaos. All the places I could go. I was amazed by everything I had never seen and the existence of so many paths was liberating, as it was to know I could choose not to follow any of them, and to just remain on the beaten track. To just stay put.

Through those windows I saw the possibility of just accepting work and my career as they are, sometimes important, sometimes trivial. Of trying to connect with some sense of purpose across other aspects of my life—perhaps every aspect of my life. Of living more holistically. Experimenting with different things, getting back to writing, reconnecting with the creative self that was for very long suppressed by the stress of the corporate world. Rediscovering.

And I observed in myself the unshakable human ability to adapt and to find some type of genuine pleasure in anything. Absolutely any activity and context, really, if we are able to put things in the right perspective.

I began trying to contemplate my concerns with my physical appearance with an increasing awareness, self-respect and love, and to force myself to wonder what I actually like to look like. Rediscovering my most intimate understanding of beautiful, of attractive, of self-satisfaction, of sexy. Asking myself, what does that mean?

For the very first time I thought about what I enjoy in other people, and what I enjoy in being with other people. About what I want from those around me and the possibilities and limitations of what I am able to give them back. I exercise with positioning myself openly to all types of people in my life, putting myself out there and hearing back. With building true, bespoke human engagement, rather than following playbooks and unspoken expectations.

Out of these windows I see people in peace with themselves and with others. They go about their lives filled with love and respect, they like difference, novelty, weirdness and they get bored easily. They look at other people with interest and curiosity, and mix and mingle, come together and drift apart with lightness and grace. They are free. Their problems are theirs, and not others', and they face them with honesty and courage. They don't judge, don't make assumptions, don't take for granted, and that's what makes them peaceful—happy.

When I allow myself to look out at those windows I play with reality and dream of futures I've never seen or heard of, of lives I never imagined even existed. I plug possibilities in and out of all aspects of my life and come up with crazy scenarios, envisioning everything that it may one day be, or that it may never be. When I look out I see roads sometimes filled with struggles, sometimes unrealistically blissful. When I look out I feel less responsible and more empowered. I feel wild. I feel childish—and in a way I think that feeling is freedom.

. . .

Can we ever become truly free? Entirely? Is it possible to live exclusively by the laws of our unique, individual nature, to put everything else aside?

Our internal changes and the things we observe shape and reshape how we view the world constantly. Both our individual psyche and living socially are incredibly complex. We are inconsistent. Restless. And we are engaged creatures, responsive to the living experience. The things we feel, see and hear change not only how we behave, but they change our essence. That essence we should listen to and celebrate. It is not a sacred gemstone, rigid and protected somewhere safe from the world outside. It is flowing living energy, constantly absorbing from life and transforming our views, our values, our expectations. Within, we evolve, change continuously. Our understanding, our taste, our motivations mature. Outside, as we walk through life, our path evolves. People come and go, the values of those around us transform as well.

So it is not only that our priorities change as we age and develop different needs—the world also changes. It starts offering new possibilities, turning down others, and, by force of human nature, we adapt. I believe entirely that we must listen to ourselves more, but our *selves* do not exist separately from the world and those around us. We are in constant symbiosis, giving and taking from the social contexts in which we are inserted. Just by starting to determine which of your values are internal, and which are assimilated, you can easily acknowledge that we often don't know where one ends and the other begins. The world remakes us, and we remake the world around us.

I had somewhat succeeded in managing my obsession with exercising, and the weird feeling of guilt I had if, for whatever reason, I failed to. And while feeling less anxious and more comfortable with myself, I noticed that I still missed the physical effort, sweating. I also observed that I intimately, genuinely liked what I saw in the mirror when I kept active. Could it be that the aesthetic standards are so internalized that they get to influence my natural responses, or are some of those preferences actually mine? Had they become mine? Or when it comes to money: it is objectively great to have it. The things it can buy make us feel good. Intimately, not by their visibility. And yet its importance is determined externally. Our social context will influence how much we think we need. To what extent does our ambition come from our legitimate search for pleasure and self-satisfaction, and when does it become yet another—perhaps today's greatest—socially-determined measure of value? We can't ever tell.

Living in our own way is complex because our way incorporates others' ways, and then changes again. So it's impossible to know. Our essence is social. What I try to listen for is to any potential disconnect between what I intake and my gut. My pursuits and my heart. I try to remind myself of who I (currently think I) am, and what I (think I) want, and go in constant effort to get closer to my ever-evolving essence. But that is hardly straightforward because I never *am,* objectively, but rather always *become*. So, despite the constant effort, the ongoing movement towards my own heart, connecting with it in its pure form doesn't seem like a possibility. Does that mean all our efforts towards freedom mean nothing and are inevitably wasted?

Eduardo Galeano was a Uruguayan poet and revolutionary, and his most-celebrated work, *Open Veins of Latin America,* inspired the resistance and the fight against fascism and authoritarian regimes across the continent in the 20th century. He dedicated his work and life to the heritage, the memories, and the true independence of the continent, but his quest was never entirely fulfilled; the Latin America he envisioned is still a dream, his fight is still relevant, and is still being fought, even years after his death. Did he resent the lack of accomplishment?

He replied with the story of a friend of his, Argentinian filmmaker Fernando Birri, who was once asked by a student: "What is the purpose of utopia?" Birri replied that utopia lies out at the horizon. If we walk two steps, it takes two steps further. If we walk ten steps, the horizon moves ahead another ten. We can never reach it, no matter how hard we try. So what is the purpose of utopia? It is for us to walk.

Only ever accessing drives, wishes and tastes that have been tinged by our social experience is not a reason for not reaching out to them at all. And ultimately, the world's consensuses, tradition, the things we learn are not bad things. They are, indeed, part of ourselves; they are also our own. The self alone does not evolve in the same way, it is exhilarating to be part of this dynamic where we are able to both learn and shape what *normal* is and what it becomes.

I now look at my family's habits, their traditions, their everyday lives with a kind of interest of belonging. I feel connected, though not attached. I recognize origin, and not boundaries. We can love to be alone, and then learn it might be nice to be together. We can appreciate professional development, knowledge, power. Those feelings become, indeed, our own. We cannot help being influenced, but we can resist being controlled.

What I've been exercising is not rebellion—as much as I am fond of the idea in itself. I have been exercising awareness. Pure, simple awareness. That is my wholehearted suggestion: I invite you to look at your frustrations, the things that make you unhappy. The gap between where you are, and where you wish you were. What you seem to think are your failures, anything in your life that doesn't make you happy. Think about them and assess if they are really yours. Observe if they connect to things that you intimately appreciate or wish for, or if somehow, they are things everyone else seems to have or want.

Contemplate the infinitude of your possibilities, not only in the terms you've been used to—changing jobs or city—but in your own terms. They are limitless. Think of the world as a playground where anything, everything can be. It just takes looking outside the windows.

The world, our families, friends, the media will never stop setting standards, laying down their rules, establishing guidelines. Be, eat, buy, do, don't. Belong. And because of the dynamic between us and them, between the self and the world, our immersion and exchange, we will inevitably follow some of them. Their values will be our values. They may even satisfy us, eventually. There is no way to know.

EPILOGUE

You could ask, but if our nature cannot be delimited, if it's fluid and blurry, tainted and not pure, can we ever be truly free? I don't think so, not entirely. Because the boundaries become us, they become part of ourselves. Nevertheless, the only way to be happy might be to keep endlessly trying.

ACKNOWLEDGMENTS

I've been very lucky, through the years, to come across individuals and ideas that helped me understand my feelings and my thinking time and again. A human full of frustrations, insecurities and fear, and a hopeless overthinker, I have always refused to either accept or overcome my angst and have instead kept endlessly wondering 'why?' And I noticed that whenever I was searching for answers, instead of providing solutions, life inspired me to keep asking more questions.

Other people's experiences—things I read, concepts I was taught or anecdotes I heard—always helped me articulate and move forward with my reflections and my understanding of life, and they are the backbone of this essay. While I tried to untangle my restlessness through the years, I came across seemingly disconnected thoughts and examples that built up like a mosaic, with precision. My own history, theoretical concepts on human nature, and real-life stories, together assembling a portrait of life. A few specific people, intentionally or not, guided my thinking and helped glue the pieces together.

My former psychotherapist Jose Augusto, who first opened my eyes to the importance of my idiosyncrasies and individuality. They are the basis for the healthy discomfort that keep me challenging normality, again and again, every time the world somehow tried to impose standards, expectations and ways of living.

My current psychotherapist, Joaquim, who constantly opens my eyes to life's many possibilities and to the need to build my own path. This idea was crucial for me to start noticing what were my own drivers and those I took in from the rest of the world.

Bhante Kovida and Bhante Pannavamsa, monks at the London Buddhist Vihara and guides on my spiritual journey, who introduced me to Buddhist philosophy. The concepts of compassion and equanimity triggered me to wonder why we look at some people with admiration and others with aversion; some with interest, and others with disdain. Through those lenses, I realized that we judge others based on the same standardized, meaningless attributes that we use to judge ourselves, and forget that the other, too, has their individuality and the right not to conform.

BIBLIOGRAPHY

ABRAMOVIC, Marina, and James Kaplan. Walk through Walls: A Memoir. New York, 2017.

BARASH, David P. Myth of Monogamy. Freeman, 2001.

BAUMAN, Zygmunt. Consuming Life. Cambridge: Polity Press, 2008.

BAYLEY, Stephen. Taste: The Secret Meaning of Things. London: Circa Press, 2018.

BONDER, Nilton. Our Immoral Soul: A Manifesto of Spiritual Disobedience. Boston: Shambhala, 2014.

CAMUS, Albert, and Justin OBrien. The Myth of Sisyphus. New York: Vintage International, 2018.

COELHO, Paulo. O Zahir. Rio de Janeiro: Rocco, 2005.

DUBOIS, Philippe. "Trace-Image to Fiction-Image: The Unfolding of Theories of Photography from the 80s to the Present." October 158 (2016): 155-66. doi:10.1162/octo_a_00275.

ECO, Umberto. On Beauty: A History of a Western Idea. London: MacLehose Pres, 2010.

ECO, Umberto. On Ugliness. New York: Rizzoli, 2011.

ECO, Umberto. The Open Work. Cambridge: Harvard University Press.

GOFFMAN, Erving. The Presentation of Self in Everyday Life. New York: Anchor Books, 2008.

WOOLF, Virginia. A Writer's Diary. New York: Mariner Books, 2003.

LISPECTOR, Clarice. Perto do coração selvagem: romance. Rio de Janeiro: Rocco, 1998.

LISPECTOR, Clarice. Uma aprendizagem, ou, O livro dos prazeres: romance. 18. ed. Rio de Janeiro: Nova Fronteira, 1988.

MILL, John Stuart. A system of logic: ratiocinative and inductive: being a connect view of the principles of evidence and the methods of scientific investigation. London: Longmans, Green and Co., 1956

SPINOZA, Benedictus De, E. M. Curley, and Stuart Hampshire. Ethics. London: Penguin Books, 2005.

TZU, Sun. The Art of War. Pax Librorum Pub. H, 2009.

CPSIA information can be obtained
at www.ICGtesting.com
Printed in the USA
BVHW041801120519
548076BV00011B/182/P